Meaningful Translation:
Its Implications for the Reader

United Bible Societies
Monograph Series

UBS Monograph Series, No. 5

Meaningful Translation:
Its Implications for the Reader

Johannes P. Louw, Editor

UNITED BIBLE SOCIETIES
Reading, UK
New York

© 1991, United Bible Societies
UBS Monograph 5
ISBN 0-8267-0455-7
Printed in the United States of America
ABS-10/02-100-600—Yu1(3)-104761

CONTENTS

Introduction

The large variety of languages spoken in Africa along with the many diverse cultures involved in, and even overlapping some of these languages, make the continent of great importance to translators.

In 1985 the Bible Society of South Africa organized a convention of translators to pay special attention to the problems receptors so often encounter in understanding a translated text. Sponsored by the Bible Society of South Africa, translators representing various languages from the southern African subcontinent (see p. 97) convened in Pretoria under the auspices of the Institute for Interlingual Communication at the University of Pretoria to discuss and to share aspects of translating with emphasis on how receptors react to Bible translations. This volume illustrates some of the important issues especially in terms of the receptor (whether hearer or reader) and the intelligibility of Bible translations.

The content and ideals of this convention, which also served as a training workshop, prompted the eventual writing of this book. Issues which seemed to be crucial in producing a really meaningful translation are presented in this book with special reference to the implications they have for the reader. Chapter 1 is primarily concerned with the nature of receptor response, while chapter 2 intends to emphasize and illustrate the so important feature of cultural presuppositions that may hamper a proper understanding of the message. Some of the sample passages selected and studied are given in chapters 3-5. These have been drafted in such a way that certain overlapping features have been discussed in either the Old or the New Testament examples in order to avoid unnecessary repetition. Therefore, chapter 3 contains more guidelines for practical procedures than chapters 4 and 5, while the latter two focus somewhat more on syntactic and semantic structures. Nevertheless, all the sample studies intend to suggest a methodology that should be taken seriously in order to avoid translating a passage without properly understanding the crucial issues that can involve misunderstanding by the hearer or reader of a translated text.

The chapters of this book have been written by the lecturers at this convention on the basis of the joint discussions with the various participating translation teams during both the theoretical and practical sessions, and contain the results of research and experience in Bible translation in Africa over a number of years.

Johannes P. Louw

Chapter 1

Bible Translation and Receptor Response

Johannes P. Louw

In translating any text one naturally has to pay close attention to the text as such. The form, setting, style, vocabulary, level of communication and many other items pertaining to the text itself are no doubt part of what a translator has to analyze very carefully in order to produce a faithful translation. In itself this observation contains nothing new. The same may be said about the acceptability of a translation. The response of the receptors, whether readers or hearers, is likewise a feature any translator will acknowledge as extremely important if the message of the original text is to be transferred meaningfully into another language. Therefore, the well known warning is generally taken seriously by translators, namely, that a translator should not so much aim at producing a translation that can be easily understood by receptors, but rather the aim should be to produce a rendering that will avoid any misunderstanding of the message by the receptors. Unless a text is quite confusing, receptors are usually able to make some sense of it. This is a remarkable human capacity. However, this ability of readers or hearers is, in fact, one of the most detrimental to translators. Therefore, the response of receptors to a translated text—and for that matter to any text—is of vital importance.

However, in some circles of Bible readers there is presently a growing resistance to dynamic or functional translations. A contention often voiced in this respect holds that a more literal translation is to be preferred, since the reader needs to see the form and structure of the original text reflected in the translation in order to be sure that the translator has not incorporated, as it is often said, personal understandings of the source text into the translation. "We will figure out what the meaning is, let the translator give us the text as it stands" occurs more than often in reactions to modern translations. This is especially serious in the case of the numerous metaphorical expressions found in the Bible. It is often claimed that dynamic translations obscure the true biblical imagery. In a recent public discussion of the matter it was alarming to realize how strongly the point was taken by well-educated people. These persons seemed to be more inclined to believe that the Bible must be rendered as close as possible to the actual form and manner of expression of the original text, since they are competent, they claim, to read any text and to understand it.

Though in some instances people prefer to use older literal translations because they have in their personal understanding come to conclusions that fit in well with their own theology, many others do have sufficient examples at hand to show how some of the modern translations are misleading even though these translations claim to have taken the original message seriously and have tried to render the real meaning of the source text as faithfully as possible. Perhaps one of the main reasons for this controversy lies in the fact that many modern translations have taken meaning seriously without sufficient care to avoid misunderstanding on the part of the receptor. Translators can very easily assume that since the rendering produced by themselves is, in their opinion, as crystal clear as one can possibly wish, no receptor will ever misunderstand the meaning. Unfortunately the problem of understanding remains, since reading a text always involves an interpretation of the text at hand. This is a very important point, for it involves the fact that even when one reads a text in one's own language, the text has to be analyzed and interpreted. We are all translators for that matter. Reading a text in one's own language is nothing less than translating the text for oneself, since one's reading entails the grouping of phrases, assigning meanings to the words and expressions of the text, observing stylistic arrangements and trying to grasp the intention of the text.

Perhaps the most crucial issue for reader's response in terms of these aspects is the nature of language. It is not merely a matter of failure to understand the nature of translation, but more basically, it is also the tendency to misunderstand the nature of language and of communication that determine the response of receptors. Once people have become aware of how language relates to experience and to interaction between participants in a communication act, the problems of a translation become much more intelligible and acceptable.

In the first place, life consists of an infinite variety of objects, events, and related features. But a language simply cannot operate efficiently if it has to have a separate word for all of these unique entities, events, and abstractions. There simply must be ways in which words can refer to classes of objects. That means that there must be some means for lumping entities into groups. There are, for example, thousands of different shapes, forms, and types of chairs, but it would be utterly useless to have a completely different word for every slightly different chair. Similarly, the human eye can distinguish fourteen million different colors and shades, but most languages get along quite well with ten to a dozen basic color terms. Similarly, there are many different kinds of flowing water in nature, but in English most people seem to get along satisfactorily with such terms as *rivulet, brook, stream, creek,* and *river.*

Not only do all languages segment and classify experience by means of words, but a high percentage of the meanings of these words have "fuzzy edges," that is, indistinct boundaries. For example, how big does a *cup* have to be before it becomes a *mug*? Or how small does a *cup* have to be before it becomes a *demitasse*? There are no fixed boundaries for *cup*, *mug*, and *demitasse*. In reality, these form a kind of continuum. In the central areas of reference the designations are clear and people readily agree about usage, but on the boundaries there may be quite different kinds of judgments as to what a particular object should be called.

Not only is there a problem of segmentation and classification of the designative meanings of words, but the same occurs with grammatical structures. Consider, for example, the following grammatical series: *his car*, *his work*, *his son*, *his arm*, *his punishment*, and *his god*. In traditional grammatical analyses, all of these expressions are called "possessive," because they are nouns preceded by a so-called possessive pronoun *his*. But the relationships between the two components "A" and "B" are certainly not always a matter of possession. In the first instance, one may, of course, define the relationship between *his* and *car*, as meaning "A owns B." But in *his work* the meaningful relationship is "A does B." In the phrase *his son* "A is biologically related to B," and in *his arm* "B is a part of A." For the phrase *his punishment*, the meaning is "A experiences B." But in *his god* the relationship may be defined either as "A worships B" or "B protects and cares for A." Just to say that all of these phrases belong to a "possessive construction" is certainly misleading. But a language would be terribly inefficient if for every possible relationship there had to be a separate construction.

One of the interesting features of language is that one can say one thing, but mean something entirely different. In fact, irony seems to be a universal phenomenon of language. In Mark 7.9, for example, Jesus is quoted as saying, "You have a fine way of rejecting God's law in order to maintain your own teaching." Jesus is not praising the Pharisees for the manner in which they circumvented the commandment to honor their parents. By the use of irony, however, the statement by Jesus becomes even more effective than a plain denunciation would have been.

Since language so frequently reflects the concepts and patterns of bahavior of a culture, one must expect similar phrases to have quite different meanings in diverse cultures. In Luke 18.13 the tax collector "beat his breast" as a way of indicating sorrow for his sins. But in a number of languages of Africa, a phrase meaning "to beat the breast" normally means "to congratulate oneself." In Ezekiel 6.11 the phrase "clap your hands and stamp your feet" would seem to suggest pleasure and delight. In reality, however, it is a symbol of foreboding of great evil to come upon the people of Israel.

On every level of language (words, grammar, and rhetoric) everything about language carries meaning. Language is a system of signs, and all the signs and arrangements of signs point to referents, whether entities, events, features, or relations. Languages do not differ essentially in what they can communicate, but in how the communication takes place. What can be said in one language can be said in a functionally equivalent manner in another language. But because languages differ in the way in which they divide up experience and in the ways in which they organize verbal signs, no two expressions in any two languages are absolutely identical in meaning. The same applies to synonymous expressions in one and the same language. All these factors are basic to hampering understanding. In fact, it is indeed remarkable that people do sometimes understand correctly if one considers the large variety of features involved in language communication. The reader or hearer always has to interpret an utterance, and therefore misunderstanding will ever be possible.

Therefore, meaningful translation has to take cognisance of the response of the receptors, although this very fact is also contested by readers who prefer to use literal translations for the reasons explained above. An objection often put forward in this respect claims that the Word of God has to be rendered as such without any consideration for the reader, since this latter regard may involve the risk of pleasing the reader and thus distorting the message in order to meet the reader's whims. This is missing the point. Receptor response is not a matter of what the reader or hearer would find pleasing—not at all! It is simply a matter of understanding, and therefore a factor any translator should keep in mind in order to avoid misunderstanding by the receptor. As such it is one of the most important tests a translator should apply to determine whether the translated text is really a meaningful translation.

In order to appreciate some of the presuppositions held by people who find it unnecessary to stress the need for a translation procedure that aims at avoiding misunderstanding, a number of reasons for resisting meaningful translation should be considered. Perhaps one of the most important is that in many cases earlier translations of the Scriptures have predisposed people to think that a translation of the Bible cannot really be understood. Sometimes this obscurity in Bible translations is justified by saying that all religious language is bound to be mysterious. Many people actually insist that religious truth is so basically incomprehensible for the human mind that a translation of the Scriptures should be equally obscure and even mystifying.

In other cases people object to a new and more meaningful translation of the Scriptures because they are too familiar with traditional ones. They may have even memorized large portions of such texts employing old-fashioned language. Therefore, any alterations seem to be either suspect or unnecessary.

Sometimes translation helpers are told that the Greek and the Hebrew texts of the Bible say such-and-such, and they assume that they must force their own languages into this Greek or Hebrew mold, even when the results are quite unnatural in, for example, an African language. The real issue, of course, is not what the Greek or Hebrew text literally "says" but what it actually "means."

Perhaps one of the most important reasons for people objecting to meaningful Scripture translations derives from their experience in learning a foreign language in a classroom. Teachers usually insist that students produce literal translations so that their comprehension of the meaning of individual words and grammatical constructions can be immediately checked. Cultural and literal considerations would hardly be taken account of within such a framework. This method of teaching a foreign language is most unfortunate, for it tends to give students a wrong impression of a foreign language, and at the same time tends to degrade a student's appreciation for his own language through the process of "butchering" it, in order to make it conform to patterns of a foreign language. Nevertheless, as a result of classroom experience in learning a foreign language, many people assume that all translations must be more or less word-for-word, and hence both unnatural and awkward.

Many readers instinctively fear new translations of the Bible because they believe that such translations are bound to "change the Bible." In reality, however, it is usually the receptor language which has undergone change, and a new translation is designed to recapture the true meaning of the Greek and Hebrew texts so that the meaning of the originals may be preserved.

Perhaps a more pervasive and yet more subtle reason for resistance to meaningful translations of the Scriptures reflects the fact that religion tends to look back rather than ahead. This is especially true of Christianity, which is rooted in a distinctive history. Therefore, the events which took place two or three thousand years ago are extremely important, when viewed from the distinctive perspective of God's entrance into history, not only in the life of Israel, but especially so in the life of ministry of Jesus. This backward look tends to be conservative, not only in theological orientation, but also in matters of language. Thus for many people, an antiquated type of language seems to imply greater authority or at least greater psychological proximity to the ancient events.

A further factor which accounts for resistance to new translations is the insecurity of leaders who may not be able to explain to laymen precisely why certain changes have been made in the text of a new translation. Without a knowledge of Greek and Hebrew, it is not easy to realize that certain changes result from differences of manuscript evidence, others from different interpretations of the text, and still others from differences of style.

To some extent prooftext preaching tends to increase resistance to meaningful translations, since preachers often concentrate on a limited number of key verses, and any alteration of these verses seems to imply a heretical tendency. The problems become even more acute when such verses are taken out of context, as in the case of Ezekiel 18.4, "the soul that sins shall die." The context clearly indicates that this verse is not designed as a statement of fatalism but means that a child is not to die because of the sins of the father nor is a father to be punished for the sins of a child. In other words, each individual is responsible for his or her own conduct and is to be judged accordingly. It is a statement of caution to admonish and to call for proper conduct.

At times, some readers seem to take such pleasure in having difficult expressions in the Scriptures explained that one might assume that preaching involves exegeting awkwardly translated passages. In reality, however, the preacher's task is to take the clear message of the Scriptures and to apply this message to the circumstances of present-day life. Therefore, meaningful translation paves the way to meaningful application.

Though in the past, translators have indeed been concerned to some extent about the reader of the Scriptures, too little attention was given to the hearer. Receptors are not only readers but also hearers. This is especially vital in Africa. Many receptors of the Scriptures in Africa have learned the message through hearing, especially in listening to Bible reading in church. It is a remarkable capacity that many Africans have, namely, an incredible auditory memory. Translating the Bible in Africa entails a thorough consideration for this fact. It asks more of a translator. If the meaning of a text is not immediately clear to a reader, he or she can look back and forward to see just how the various words fit together. Concepts can be pondered, studied and reviewed. Hearers, however, must be able to grasp the meaning of a text almost immediately. This emphasis on the hearer is an important dimension to be added to our principles and procedures of Bible translation.

This book intends to highlight two areas which are of crucial importance to be carefully considered in preparing a translation that would meet the needs of readers and hearers. The one pertains to social issues, the other to literary matters. Chapter two deals primarily with the former in showing how important cultural equivalences and inequivalences need to be taken into account in the process of message transmission. Chapters three to five intend to alert the translator to his or her own understanding of the text as a literary document. Too often translators tend to plunge right into the source text and take care of various exegetical matters as the translation process develops. It is imperative for a translator to thoroughly study the source text, especially in terms of cultural and literary matters, to ensure a proper understanding of the message before any attempt is made at specifically putting one's hand to writing down a translation. The translator cannot avoid causing the receptor not to misunderstand a translated text without being quite sure that the translator's own understanding is not inadequate.

There is also another very important factor which can help readers or hearers to understand correctly, namely, the physical presentation of a translation. This entails the format and style of the printed text. For example, a format based on sense lines reflecting basic rhythmic units such as in one of the recent Zulu translations has proved to be extremely valuable in aiding understanding. Style and format involves so much that a separate monograph is currently in preparation to illustrate this important factor.

There are also other factors that can be considered, such as putting the message into poetic or singable form. This has been done effectively for the Tzeltals of Oxchuc in Southern Mexico.

Surely much more will be researched in future. Ensuring a proper understanding of the message is by far not yet exhausted. Whatever is suggested requires a full scale investigation and report. Therefore, this volume will deal only with the two areas referred to above, since these areas may be the most relevant at this stage to deal with the important issue of the literal-dynamic controversy.

This twin goals of translating, whether for biblical or secular material, are usually said to be intelligibility and acceptability. During the greater part of this century the focus has been upon intelligibility. Can people understand? If they can, will they understand correctly? Therefore, in terms of the receptor, intelligibility should be understood within the framework of the contention set forth in the discussion above: translation should not aim at producing a rendering that people can understand, but rather producing a rendering that will cause people not to misunderstand the message. Likewise acceptability needs to be understood within a new frame of reference—not merely the quality of the translation based upon its readability, and whether the style is pleasing. The element of figurative language which is so basic to all languages and all significant communicative events should not be overlooked. Acceptability should rather be judged on the basis of what is meaningful, and void of possible misunderstanding in the realm of the local receptor culture. Only in this way can people really relate to the message. If people find in a translation expressions and patterns which they can recognize as distinctive of their own culture, there is a much higher degree of intellectual and emotive identification with the message.

Chapter 2

Culture and the Form/Function Dichotomy in the Evaluation of Translation Acceptability

Ernst R. Wendland

In this chapter we wish to focus upon the issue of acceptability in translation, particularly as this relates to the matter of cultural (in) equivalence during the process of message transmission. To be specific, the question is this: how does the translator determine whether or not he has gone too far in the direction of either literal correspondence (i.e., SL[1] bias) or cultural adaptation (i.e., RL[2] bias)? What, then, are some of the pertinent criteria that can help him to determine the answer to this question in any given instance? In short, how does he go about evaluating his own translation? We might summarize the key aspects of this issue by reproducing a diagram taken from chapter 7 of *Language, Society and Bible Translation* (p. 218, which may be read in conjunction with the present discussion).

(focus on)	Meaning	Form
SL	FIDELITY	PROXIMITY
RL	INTELLIGIBILITY	IDIOMATICITY

The four variables of fidelity, intelligibility, idiomaticity, and proximity may be briefly related to the parameters of language focus on the one hand (i.e., SL or RL), and message focus on the other (i.e., form or meaning) as follows: *Fidelity* is concerned with the accurate transmission of the sense of the SL text (with

---

[1] SL = source language.

[2] RL = receptor language.

regard to both content and function) as intended by the original author. *Intelligibility* concentrates on the comprehensibility of the message in the RL, namely, is the average receptor generally able to understand the translation, or are there a significant number of places where misunderstanding occurs for one reason or another? *Idiomaticity* pertains to the naturalness of the linguistic forms that have been used in the translation; the text should not give evidence of a "foreign accent" as far as the language itself is concerned. *Proximity*, then, takes into consideration the form of the message in the SL and the need to preserve, whenever possible, the integrity and distinctiveness of the original in matters relating to the biblical historical and cultural setting.

Now these four criteria are not isolated aspects of the translation process. On the contrary, they are very closely related and must therefore be treated as a complex set of mutually interdependent factors when assessing any given piece of text for acceptability, from the individual word right up to a complete discourse. The purpose of this chapter is to demonstrate the importance of adopting such a perspective as a basic procedural principle when setting up a Bible translation program. There is widespread agreement nowadays regarding the criteria of fidelity and intelligibility, and so we will concentrate our attention on the other two, especially since it is in this area that the cultural factor becomes crucially relevant to the discussion. Of particular concern is the matter of the use of "cultural substitutes" in the RL, for here is where the twin concerns of proximity and idiomaticity so frequently come into direct conflict.

It is important to consider the problem of lexical inequivalence between SL and RL primarily in terms of solutions, namely, the various techniques that are available for handling such difficulties in translation. Our goal is to suggest a heuristic procedure for examining in more detail the concepts behind the surface forms, or words of the original text, in order to specify more precisely, if possible, the nature of the various types of cultural incongruence that arise when we attempt to render these same concepts in the receptor language. For along with a more accurate determination of the problem involved often comes a more suitable solution, that is, a way of dealing with the difficulty which better expresses the communicative intent of the original message. We shall use the old and new translations in both Chichewa and Chitonga (i.e., of Central Africa) to illustrate a number of factors which can help one to measure the amount of distortion in form and/or function that results from a literal rendering as compared with a cultural adaptation in specific biblical contexts. The aim is to work toward a method of evaluating the pros and cons of alternative translational possibilities in this area.

Just as lexical items may be broken down into various components of meaning (see Nida, 1975; Louw, ed., 1985), so also one might analyze certain discrete aspects of social life and behavior in a similar way. Componential analysis is a comparative process, and while it is often helpful to study related objects and practices within the same culture (e.g., the various types of sacrifice prescribed by the Mosaic Law), it often is more necessary from the point of view of translation to compare superficially corresponding but functionally dissimilar features of the environment and patterns of behavior that exist between different peoples, namely, those of Bible times and receptors today. Alternatively, it is also profitable to examine the way in which different types of articles and activities, i.e., as manifested in the SL and RL cultures, may in fact perform the same, or at least a similar, purpose in their respective societies. The ability, then, to differentiate between similarities and differences with respect to form and/or function is a vital part of the analytical process.

There are thus features that one cultural form, whether verbal or nonverbal, shares with another comparable (i.e., potentially replaceable) form with regard to their significance as signs in a particular social and/or linguistic setting. These are the "common" components of meaning. There are other features which serve to distinguish and differentiate one form from another. These are the "diagnostic" components of meaning. The features, or components, themselves may be of two principal types. One type of meaningful behavior may be either the same as or different from another with respect to:

a)   FORM - the perceptible, surface features of a given culture, both material (e.g., tools, pottery, clothing, art forms, etc.) or nonmaterial (e.g., ceremonies, rituals, social institutions, words, grammatical constructions, songs, etc.).

b)   FUNCTION - the reason, purpose, goal, or motivation behind any cultural phenomenon as this relates to the basic needs of the individual or society as a whole (i.e., physical, psychological, interpersonal, or spiritual).

The sum total of these various attributes and significations constitutes the "meaning" of the object or event as perceived by its users/agents/experiencers/observers, etc. This includes the various associations that are connected with it, i.e., the attitudes, values, connotations, feelings, impressions, etc. which are attached to a particular cultural form in the minds of the members of society. It is a meaning which is culturally determined and which, therefore, can only in rare instances be transferred intact to a different cultural context. That is to say, custom X in Hebrew society, for example, will normally differ from custom Y in Chewa society with regard to one or more of the associated characteristics of form and/or function. The task of the translator, then, is to evaluate the relative importance of these differences as they relate to the several possibilities for rendering the SL practice in the RL. His aim is to achieve the closest, natural communicative equivalent in the RL. He frequently finds himself in a position where each of the potential RL solutions has some features in common with the original form while other features are different to varying degrees. A final decision must oftentimes be made on the negative basis of which translation possibility is likely to distort the SL meaning the *least* or to cause the least misunderstanding for the receptor group.

The continuum of variation between perfect equivalence in form and function between the SL and the RL item and complete inequivalence may be arbitrarily broken up for the sake of comparison into four distinct nodes as shown below:

$$(+FO/+FU)-----(+FO/-FU)-----(-FO/+FU)-----(-FO/-FU)$$

These points, or better, areas of differentiation, are described and exemplified in the discussion which follows.

It is always encouraging to encounter at least a few close correspondences along one's way through the Bible—with regard to connotative associations and situational usage as well as basic form and function (i.e., +FO/+FU). The Chewa translator will undoubtedly find more than his European counterpart as he proceeds through the Old Testament. These cover the whole range of both verbal and nonverbal symbolic behavior, e.g., the importance of an adult male's name being remembered through his posterity (2 Sm 14.7) and the curse of childlessness (Gn 30.23); reference to the dog as being an image of some despised and wretched creature (2 Sm 3.8); the official rite of installing a king into office by anointing his head with oil (1 Sm 10.1, though there is a slight shift in form here from olive [Hebrew] to castor bean [Chewa] oil); the practice of a diviner employing an initial revelation to establish his credentials (1 Sm 9.20); the taboo which prohibits men from having sexual relations with their wives during times of crucial importance to the community at large—a hunting or military expedition (1 Sm 21.4-5) or preceding great religious events (Ex 19.15). The similarity in total meaning can even be as culturally specific (Tonga) as the measurement of a piece of land—a "yoke"—by the amount of plowing that a team (or "yoke") of oxen can complete in a single day (1 Sm 14.14), or in the form of a particular "praise name" for God, e.g., *Munamazuba* 'one-of-the-tribe-of-days' (Tonga) for the "Ancient of Days" referred to in Dn 7.22.

At times, as noted above, the correspondence is virtually the same, except for a slight difference in formal properties, e.g., the "dung" referred to in Zp 1.17

was specifically globular in form (as that of camels and sheep, from the Hebrew root 'to roll'), but the word is rendered in Tonga as "cattle manure," which has a rather different shape, but certainly a similar connotation. Instead of "weeds among the wheat" (Mt 13.25), the "enemy" of Christ's parable sows "false sugar cane" (*misonde*, Tonga) in a field of *maila* 'cereal grain' (used generically here), for literal *nsaku* 'weeds' are readily distinguished from the food crop and they don't burn very easily (v. 40). *Misonde*, on the other hand, is almost indistinguishable from *maila* until the grain matures and, when dry, it burns up quickly. The "wild cucumbers" (in Tonga *basijatwa* 'the untouchable ones') probably resemble the "wild gourds" that Elisha's servant picked out in the field (2 Kg 4.39), but the important thing is that they have the same effect if eaten, i.e., some are edible (like mushrooms), while others are not and can cause serious illness. The *lupanga* 'machete' (Chewa) is similar in form to the biblical "sword," and while the machete is not typically used as a weapon of war, it may readily be so employed; hence it is a close equivalent.

The other extreme on the Form-Function continuum is represented by those cases where there is no matching of either form or function, i.e., the concept is completely foreign to the world-view of life of the receptor culture (-FO/-FU). Fortunately, this situation is not too common, but there will always be several notable instances where real conceptual difficulties are involved. This occurs most often with certain technical terms that pertain to specific aspects of the SL culture, e.g., centurion, tribune, Pharisee, demon, angel, Sheol, sabbath, ephod, breastplate, baptism, and birthright. The description of God as being a "spirit" (Jn 4.24), to give a more fundamental example, is a problem in many (not all) Bantu cultures. The word for "spirit" in these languages always implies an essential element of humanness, i.e., ancestral spirit. The notion of death, too, is present, for no one becomes a "spirit" until he/she has passed the threshold of the grave. The associated attribute of "holiness" is also a difficult idea to convey when applied either to God or the things of God. The deity—and all Central African peoples acknowledge only one, though he may be referred to by a number of different names and praise appellations—is already one of a kind and thus set apart from man. This is a basic presupposition, one that is simply taken for granted, and thus God's "holiness" does not need to be represented referentially by a lexical item (just as God himself is never represented materially in the form of an idol). The state of being "purified" is an extremely important one in Bantu culture, but this is always interpreted in a human social or ritual sense (especially in a situation where a taboo has been violated), and such a concept therefore cannot be applied naturally to God. A man or woman whose spouse has died, for example, must be "cleansed" (often by a ritual act of sexual intercourse) before he/she can resume normal social activities in the community.

This often leaves God, the Holy Spirit in particular, with various designations of "whiteness/ cleanness" (Chewa), or "redness" (Tonga), to denote his "holy" being, nature, activities, and objects.

Other culturally foreign concepts may not be as crucial theologically, but they present the same difficulties for the translator, e.g., (male) "circumcision" (Gn 17, especially of a small child, Lk 1.59); "adoption" (of a son, Ga 4.5); "homosexuals" (Lv 18.22); or "male cult prostitutes" (2 Kg 23.7). The last two terms, for example, are translated respectively in Chewa by a loanword (i.e., *matanyula*, picked up by men who left Central Africa to go work in the mines of South Africa), and by a loanword plus a classifier (*mahule achimuna* 'male prostitutes'), which is really a contradiction in terms. Similarly, the only thing that can be done to render such an unheard of concept as a "eunuch" (Mt 19.12) is to form an equally strange lexical compound, *muntu muzibe* 'a man —castrated bull' (Tonga).

The great majority of translation problems, of course, fall somewhere in between the two poles of a relatively exact correspondence in formal and functional properties and complete inequivalence. One often finds, for example, that the RL can match a certain SL concept with regard to form, but the respective functions (and related associations) are significantly different (i.e., +FO/-FU). In Tonga socioreligious culture, it is not uncommon to hear that "one of God's spirits" or a "spirit from God" (i.e., possible translation glosses for the phrase *muuya wa Leza* 'spirit of God') has taken possession of someone, just as it happened to Saul (1 Sm 10.6). However, the purpose, also a beneficial one, would be for divining—to reveal the will of the spirit concerned—and not merely "dancing and shouting" (v. 10, GNB), or worse, a "furious" anger (1 Sm 11.6). Uncut hair might be the sign of a special religious habit in the OT (i.e., that of a Nazarite, Jd 13.5), but in a Central African village, only a mentally deranged person would allow his hair to grow that way. A Hebrew person's face might "grow pale" in fright (Na 2.10), but if this happened to a Mutonga, he might well be accused of being a witch! To Tonga women the prohibition against cutting "tattoo marks" in Lv 19.28 would be a very difficult one to keep, for this practice, which includes the application of special "medicine," is employed either to attract men, or to alleviate severe headaches. It has nothing to do with mourning customs as in the original. A Chewa woman, on the other hand, might incise medicine at the time of a funeral as a means of warding off the "spirit" of the diseased or at other times simply as a form of ornamentation—both, however, quite distinct functionally from the Hebrew custom. The warning "lest the land vomit you out" (Lv 18.28) strikes home to the traditional Tonga listener, for this is a major concern when one moves to a new home. The reason for such expulsion, however, is rather different from what

God was getting at in Leviticus, i.e., as a punishment for religious infidelity. Upon reaching a new location, the Tonga clan head must see to it that the place has first been freed from the control of unfriendly spirits, who could bring sickness or even death upon members of his family. The familiar NT picture of rejection, i.e., being thrown out into the "darkness" and "gnashing one's teeth" in anger (e.g., Mt 22.13), conveys quite a different connotation in a Tonga setting, where grinding teeth is associated with being cold, which is what a person would expect were he to be told to leave the evening fireplace!

And finally, there are those instances where the RL would normally (were the Bible not involved) utilize a different form in order to communicate the functional significance of the original (i.e., -FO/+FU). In most Central African contexts, for example, the man in Christ's parable who "built his house on a rock" (Mt 7.24) would be the one considered to be a "fool," for how could he possibly dig a proper foundation or holes in which to sink the support poles for his roof and to provide the framework for his walls? Similarly, the typical Tonga farmer can only shake his head in wonder at Christ's advice to "invest (his) money with the bankers" (Mt 25.27), for why should any sane person want to hand his money over to someone else for safekeeping? Rather, he would go out and buy some more cattle, for they are his "bank." The comforting image of Christ, the Good Shepherd, out in front leading his flock (Jn 10.3-4, 27) would not strike a very responsive chord among the Tonga. That would be seen as a very unwise thing to do, for he would turn around to find his flock all scattered about the bush countryside. Any herdsman knows that to keep proper track of his animals, he must follow behind after them! In the same way, it is clear—from the receptor perspective at any rate—that seeds which are planted only to "rot" (or "die") in the ground (Jn 12.24) are worse than worthless (i.e., alternatively, they could have at least been used for food). A seed can "bear much fruit" only if it manages to stay "alive" to germinate—having overcome the threat of rodents, birds, and drought.

Some SL forms, whether objects or activities, are immediately perceived as being foreign to the receptor culture, e.g., Rachel's carrying a waterpot on her shoulder (Gn 24.15), instead of on top of her head as is the practice in Central Africa—or her wearing a ring in her nose for decoration, rather than a "nose-stock" (Chewa). Other forms reveal their strangeness only after some translation testing has shown that people are consistently misunderstanding the text. To say, for example, that Jesus "loved" Martha (an adult woman, apparently unmarried) in Tonga implies a close sexual relationship (i.e., *yanda* 'love' + 'desire'). In order to avoid this unwanted implication, one has to say that he "agreed/got along well with" (*mvwana*) her. While it seems quite easy to translate the concept of "king's sceptre" (Ps 45.6) in Chewa, i.e., "the walking stick of the chief," that gives readers only the form of the original. Its function, that is, as a symbol of royal authority, would have to be conveyed by an entirely different form, namely, the chief's "flywhisk" (*mcira*, lit. 'tail'). On the other hand, the "walking stick" could be employed to designate the office of the witch-finder, or herbalist (*sing'anga*). One hardly thinks twice about a literal rendering of Job's description of his physical affliction that his "skin turns black" (Jb 30.30). An African, however, becomes "light" (or "reddish") when he is on his deathbed.

The form of entire utterances may carry unwanted associations and/or be completely inappropriate in the sociocultural context of the RL. Rachel's bitter command to Jacob, "Give me children or I die!" (Gn 30.1) sounds most peculiar in a Tonga setting since Jacob had already produced children by his other wives. Therefore, if a charge of infertility were being levelled, she herself would be the most likely suspect (in Central Africa, the "burden of proof" in such situations lies first of all with the woman in any case). On the other hand, readers could well interpret Rachel's exclamation as being a complaint against Jacob for not doing enough to solve the problem between them. But then the import of her words would have been more along the lines of a rebuke, or even an insult, intended to provoke him into taking some concrete action, such as through a visit to the local herbalist—e.g., *Tozyali* 'You are not begetting (children),' or in more colloquial terms: *Tuli bakaintu toonse mung'anda muno* 'We are both women in this house.'

The preceding examples have illustrated how the various culturally related problems that arise during translation may be analyzed for a start in general terms of form and function. We now wish to take the analysis process a step further in order to specify more fully the precise nature of the difficulty involved in a given instance. Such specification is necessary if a thorough evaluation of the different solutions is going to be made.

When seeking to resolve any instance of inequivalence in the message transfer process, the translator must be sure to carefully study both the SL and the RL contexts in order to pinpoint the potential problems as exactly as possible. It is essential, as an initial step, to determine the particular area of focus of the SL form under consideration. To summarize: in the first place, is a literal or a nonliteral reference involved? The term "literal" includes the central, or primary, meaning of a given lexical item, that is to say, the sense which first comes to mind to most people when the word (or phrase) is mentioned in isolation, i.e., without a textual or extratextual context, as well as all secondary, or extended, meanings. The latter refers to those senses which share at least one basic component of meaning with the central one. The central meaning is generally (but not always) that one which occurs most frequently in the language and which is most important from a sociocultural perspective. "Body" (Gr. *soma*), for example, refers to the entire structure and physical substance that comprises a living organism (man, animal, or plant—e.g., Mt 6.25). The word *soma*, as used in the NT, encompasses a number of secondary meanings, e.g., the corpse of a dead person (Lk 17.37) or natural objects found in the "heavens" (1 Co 15.40).

Any "literal" reference may be further distinguished according to whether there is a prevailing focus in the context upon its form or its function (as discussed above), for if both aspects cannot be conveyed naturally in a translation, then a choice between the two will have to be made. Usually it is the function which is most important, e.g., the fertility-producing properties of "mandrakes" (Gn 30.14) or the use of "teraphim" as objects of worship (Jd 18.18). There are occasions, however, when it is necessary to preserve certain of the formal features of a word's meaning, especially in the case of those terms which are of special symbolic or cultural significance in the Bible, e.g., wine (Jn 2.9), fig tree (Mk 11.20), or crown (Rv 4.10). In certain contexts, of course, both the form and the function may be in focus, e.g., cross (Jn 19.17), or necessary for understanding, e.g., phylacteries (Mt 23.5).

Nonliteral, including figurative, meanings differ from literal ones in that they do not share any major semantic components with the primary sense of a word, e.g., some of the other meanings of *soma*, denoting: one's entire self (Ro 12.1), slaves to be bought and sold (Rv 18.13), reality as contrasted with "shadow" (Cl 2.17), one's degenerate human nature (Cl 2.11), the Church as a unified group of believers (Ro 12.5), or human existence with all of its troubles (Hb 13.3). Rather, these senses are each linked to the central meaning by means of a special logical relationship, which may be of two general types: similarity (e.g., simile, metaphor) or contiguity (i.e., temporal, spatial, cause-effect, part-whole, etc.—e.g., metonymy, synecdoche).

A nonliteral meaning is often employed as a didactic, poetic, or rhetorical device—that is, to increase the impact and appeal of the message. It may, however, have a historical or an ahistorical focus. Most figures are of the latter type, that is, they bear no perceptible relation to the temporal, social, ecological, or dramatic setting in which they were first uttered. Other figures do manifest such a connection, in which case the actual form of the imagery becomes more important and hence necessary to preserve, if possible. Generally, these occur in narrative texts, including such examples as Christ's references: to "bearing fruit" in the context of the parable of the sower (Mk 4.20); to "harvest," "sowing," "reaping," "laboring," etc. when actually on the scene of a ripening grainfield (Jn 4.35-38); to "bread," "hunger," and "thirst" after he had miraculously fed a multitude with a few barley loaves (Jn 6.35); or to spiritual "sight" and "blindness" when in the company of a blind man whom he had just healed (Jn 9.39-41).

Historically-oriented figures of speech may have either a formal and/or a functional focus as mentioned above. With an ahistorical figure, there may be an emphasis on either the semantic content or the rhetorical effect in its context of use. The latter is usually the point of using a figure in the first place, but in some instances, particularly in the case of descriptions, explanations, and references with potential symbolic or religious significance, the content may be especially important, e.g., "all we *like sheep* have gone astray" (Is 53.6); "you are *the salt* of the earth" (Mt 5.13); "the Holy Spirit descended in bodily form *as a dove*" (Lk 3.22), "a sound came from heaven *like the rush of a mighty wind*" (Ac 2.2); "I am Alpha and Omega, *the first and the last*" (Rv 22.13).

The various possibilities for analyzing the critical (contextually focal) aspects of a culturally unfamiliar SL concept (object/event) are summarized on the diagram below:

There may, of course, be instances of overlapping and multiple meaning, where a given SL item involves what appear to be several mutually exclusive categories, for example, in the case of figurative actions, such as Pilate's washing his hands (literal) to declare himself innocent of Christ's death (non-literal, Mt 27.24). In other contexts a term may function simultaneously on two different levels of discourse, literal and nonliteral, such as in a parable, e.g., the sower and the seed (Mt 13). The preceding is not intended as a rigid classificatory system, but merely as a heuristic framework to help keep the major analytical considerations in view.

We turn now to the RL and an examination of how different translation possibilities may be evaluated in our search for the closest natural and functional equivalent of the original cultural form. We will focus our attention upon the middle two nodes of the form-function grid presented earlier, i.e., (+FO/ -FU) and (-FO/+FU). Each one of these hypothetical points along the continuum is associated with a particular problem in the effort to achieve equivalence in communicative value between the SL and RL messages. The first (+FO/-FU), frequently characterizes a literal translation (LT). The result of such a rendering is that four aspects, or we might say "components," of equivalence are often not realized in the communication process. The major factor is the general one relating to the "meaning" of the message. Three others are connected with the matter of idiomaticity, which was one of the four criteria distinguished earlier as being important in the activity of appraising a translation for acceptability, namely: impact, connotation, and naturalness.

The description (-FO/+FU) applies in particular to what we have been calling a "cultural substitute" (i.e., CS). This type of solution always involves a divergence, whether major or minor, from the original with respect to the generic factor of "form." There are three other aspects of the evaluative criterion of "closeness" that may also be affected by the use of a CS, namely: history, lifestyle, and worldview. These eight components of equivalence are illustrated with biblical examples below. This inventory may be employed to provide a more exact assessment of the nature and the degree of distortion that results from the use of a literal translation of the original SL form on the one hand, and the introduction of a cultural substitute in function from the receptor environment on the other. The translator's aim, of course, is to keep such deviation to a minimum with respect to the central aspects of meaning of the original as manifested in a particular context of use.

1. Form

Every cultural substitute has certain qualities that differ from the formal features of the SL item in some way. The smaller the disparity, the more acceptable the solution, as when "wild dog" (Chewa) is used for "wolf" in Mt 10.16; "stretcher" (Chewa) for "bier" in Lk 7.14; or "mat" (Chewa) for "bed" (Gr. lit., "place for reclining") in Lk 5.24. Great differences in form, on the other hand, especially when the RL referent relates to a different semantic domain than the original term, may raise questions in the minds of certain receptors, namely, those who are either familiar with the biblical setting or who notice the discrepancy when reading a different translation—if they find "pillow" (GNB) instead of "couch," for example, in Ps 6.6; "leopard" (Chewa) for "wild donkey" in Gn 16.12; or "coffin" (NIV) for "bier" in Lk 7.14. Whether or not these shifts in form are valid and/or acceptable depends on some of the other factors to be discussed below. An inappropriately placed CS may at times give the text a wrong meaning: when "grave" in 2 Kg 13.21 is rendered by *manda* in Chewa, for example, the implication is that Elisha's grave had been left unfilled with dirt since the time it was dug—truly a revolting idea to people of any culture! This grave was of course a cave (or sepulcher), and this has to be clarified by a descriptive phrase, i.e., "a cave for placing the dead inside."

An LT, on the other hand, in addition to being unnatural linguistically, may also completely distort the forms of the receptor culture in a particular context. The translation may indeed be meaningful in itself, but it gives a wrong or an inappropriate meaning in the RL sociocultural setting. For example, it would be a virtual impossibility for someone to sleep outside "on the roof" of a rural African house (1 Sm 9.25); thus even to suggest this is a grave insult. In Tonga, this problem is avoided by a generic expression, i.e., Saul's bed was prepared "up there on top." "Evildoers who *eat up* my people" (Ps 14.4) would most certainly be understood to be *mfiti* 'witches' by a majority of receptors in Central Africa. Then again, in Ne 2.8 we read about a certain Persian official who was "the keeper of the king's forest." A literal rendering in Tonga turns out as "the watcher of the trees of the chief." But since the word for "tree" also means "magical potion," which seems to fit even better in this passage, most people would take this as a reference to the royal medicine man, i.e., the one who protects the chief from witches and sorcerers.

Many idioms and "dead" figures of speech feature some very culturally-specific references, but since the form is no longer in focus (particularly if these expressions are the normal way of conveying the idea concerned), there is no real conceptual misrepresentation involved with their use, e.g., "in the heat of the day" (Gn 18.1) by the Tonga "when the sun pounds the jackal in a grain mortar"; a very "severe famine" (Gn 43.1) by "the hunger kept stirring up the dust" (Tonga - i.e., in Central Africa drought and hunger go hand in hand); ". . . in my inmost self . . . another law . . ." (Ro 7.22-23) by ". . . with a complete heart . . . another heart . . ." (Tonga - i.e., when a person is undecided, one "heart" wants one thing, his other "heart" wants something else, cp. 1 Kg 18.21); "the time has come for my departure" (2 Ti 4.6) by "the time to tie up my few little things has arrived" (Tonga - i.e., a Mutonga does not "pack," he "binds together" his baggage). One must be careful, however, that none of these idioms carry any negative associations which might be offensive to some segment of the receptor constituency. For example, one common way of referring to someone who "dies . . . wholly at ease and secure" in Tonga (Jb 21.23) is *kalifwebela* '(he dies) while smoking his pipe.' But this expression, though it is not to be taken literally, would be objectionable to those churches which prohibit their members from smoking. It would also, of course, be an anachronism.

2. Meaning

When a cultural substitute is used in the RL (just as in the case of a literal translation), it usually happens that some of the components of meaning of the SL expression are added, lost, or altered in the process of transfer. This is a relative matter, of course, since not all semantic features are equal in value or importance. But the goal is always to find the *closest* natural equivalent. For example, indigenous Chewa *mkate* 'bread' has some aspects in common with the original, i.e., it is made from flour and baked/cooked, but other qualities are quite different, e.g., the flour is maize and no yeast is used—moreover, it is eaten as a "sweet" rather than as a staple. Thus, this term presents the same problem as the loanword *buledi*, since the latter is only bought in a bakery and, being associated with a European diet, is widely viewed as a "luxury" item, at least by many government officials. The practice of *k-sh-ph* 'witchcraft' (e.g., Ex 22.18) in Hebrew society was usually associated with magical religious rites directed toward a god/idol, whereas the Chewa equivalent (*ufiti*) involves the use of magical powers and spells to injure or even kill others in the community, especially those whom the "witch" is envious of. That is clearly a significant difference in outlook, and yet there is this basic element in common that a socially-prohibited, immoral activity is concerned, one which depends for its effectiveness upon the correct manipulation of specific supernatural forces. The Hebrew concept of *zr'th* 'leprosy' was considerably broader than what the corresponding Bantu term (*khate*/Chewa, *cinsenda*/Tonga) includes as part of its reference, the former being applied to skin disorders of all sorts (Lv 13.2f.) and even to one's clothes (Lv 13.47) and dwelling place (Lv 14.33f.) There is, however, a similar underlying assumption in that this disease was a plague sent by God (see Lv 14.34, cp. the Tonga expression for advanced leprosy *mulilo wa Leza* 'the fire of God,' i.e., it is God who "burns" the afflicted person's fingers and toes off).

The problem of specificity complicates the picture. This can operate in both directions. At times the biblical term is more general than any RL equivalent, in fact, the RL may not even have a generic word available to express the concept—or set of concepts. When Christ commands a paralyzed man to "take up your *bed* and go home" (Lk 5.24), he must be rather precise in Chewa. The loanword *bedi* is out, for that implies some sort of sturdy metal/wood frame construction together with a mattress, which would have been very difficult, if not impossible to let down through the house roof with ropes (Lk 5.19). "Mat"

(NIV) is probably a more accurate rendering of the original *klinidion* (or *kline*), which, depending upon the situation, could denote any type of base for reclining, for sleeping, eating, meditating, or whatever. There are several different types of mat in Chewa, however: one made of split reeds (*mphasa*), of palm leaves (*mkeka*), an old/well-worn one (*chika*), or one used specifically for carrying someone (*machila*). Now the latter term fits well in 5.18 when the invalid is being carried by others, but not in 5.24, where Christ tells the man to pick it up himself and go home. Here the translators selected *chika*, since the man presumably had heretofore spent most of his life lying upon it.

An example of the converse, namely, where the original term is narrower in referential scope than in CS in the RL is readily found in kinship terminology. One's "father's brother," for instance, is in Tonga considered to be one's "father" and "his wife" is one's "mother" (Lv 18.14), while a person's "daughter-in-law" is his "child" (Lv 18.15). This can, of course, lead to some interesting translation problems—and some equally novel solutions, e.g., "Saul's uncle" in 1 Sm 14.50 is termed "another of Saul" in Tonga (and the reference would be perfectly clear).

The categories of form and meaning are the most general of those that apply to cultural substitutes (or, indeed, at any linguistic aspect of translation as has already been pointed out on numerous occasions). The "components" listed below may thus be regarded as subdivisions of the preceding. Since the factors involved here are so many and complex, a further categorization may be useful in helping one to delineate the complex nature of the various problems that arise in the use of a CS (as opposed to a LT or some other translation solution). These features of meaning are not mutually exclusive, and in some cases they merely represent the same issue viewed from a somewhat different perspective. This listing is not exhaustive either, but is only suggestive of some of the key aspects that may be relevant in any evaluation of the acceptability of a given CS. The first three components discussed deal with elements of SL meaning which often require a local adaptation in order to be reproduced in the RL, and which are normally lost in a literal rendering. The last three indicate some of the major kinds of meaning distortion which can occur in this process of cultural contextualization.

3. Impact

This is a crucial feature that applies to most cultural substitutes. The use of a local term instead of a generic reference, loanword, descriptive phrase, etc. always adds an element of realism and vigor to the text, of whatever type it may be.

This is especially important in passages where the original manifests a particular emphasis which some other translational possibility simply cannot duplicate. Such "dynamism" is necessary particularly where didactic or poetic texts and/or direct discourse is involved. As Rachel and Leah, for example, bitterly complain about their father Laban's attitude toward them, they say, "Are we not regarded by him as foreigners?" (Gn 31.15). This would be a natural place in Tonga to insert the idiomatic term *banasinakooma* 'children of the drummer' instead of the usual word for "foreigners," *bazwakule* 'those who come from afar.' The point is that only the stranger, if he is lost, needs to listen for the sound of drums in order to tell him which direction to travel to find help. The word thus also adds the component of being an outsider, or "left out," which is another relevant aspect of the original situational context. Reference to an indispensible item of Chewa daily life enlivens this lament of Job, "Can that which is *tasteless* be eaten without salt?" (6.6). The obvious equivalent here is *ndiwo*, the variable "relish" or "stew" which accompanies the staple pot of cooked maize flour. Without salt, the *ndiwo* simply could not perform its essential function of flavoring the meal. In order to lend a note of urgency to Yahweh's threat, "I will make your earth like bronze" (Lv 26.19), the Tonga employs a more familiar image, "your land will dry up HARD (*ntaa*, ideophone) like a rock." Similarily, Paul's admonition, "I permit no woman . . . to have authority over men" (1 Ti 2.12), strikes closer to home when phrased in culturally more specific terms: "I do not allow a woman . . . to gaze upon the heads of men" (Tonga, i.e., as if standing over them in a stance of superiority, for women traditionally kneel when addressing men in public).

A wide range of personal opinions, intentions, and attitudes which are either an explicit or an implicit part of the biblical record need to be reproduced in a translation—from a vicious insult, e.g., "You man of blood!" (2 Sm 16.7) which becomes in Chewa: "(You person of) *chirope* sickness you!" (i.e., *chirope* being a form of mental illness, often attributed to witchcraft, which causes a person to kill again and again); to a heartfelt expression of praise and admiration, ". . . lest you quench the lamp of Israel" (2 Sm 21.17), which may be rendered by a comparable Chewa idiom: ". . . you are the one whom all Israel sleeps upon." A correspondingly wide range of RL literary forms will be necessary in order to convey these functions and to duplicate the impact of the original text. One can hardly get more culturally specific—or forceful—in effective speech than through the use of a proverb, e.g., where Solomon warns his "son" against the "evil woman": "Do not desire her beauty in your heart . . ." (Pr 6.25), the Chewa equivalent is: *chikomekome cha nkhuyu, mkati muli nyerere* 'the fig looks good (to eat, but) inside there are ants." Ideophones, too, can give a very vivid receptor-oriented impression of a dramatic situation in the SL account, e.g., as the narrator describes Ahab after Naboth's refusal: "Then Ahab went back into his house angry, with pursed lips all puffed up (facial expression) *toloo* (like a cloud of dust rising high into the clear blue sky)!" (Chewa) (cp. Hebrew: "vexed and sullen").

A more literal translation having essentially the same meaning referentially would certainly be possible in most of these cases, but it just would not carry the same punch. The translator must take care not to "overdo" a text in this regard, however, for that would distort the dynamics of the Scriptures, e.g., "Jacob flew into a rage" (Gn 30.2, LB) for "Jacob's anger was kindled" (RSV); "(the angels) will prevent you from smashing on the rocks below" (Mt 4.6, LB) for "lest you strike your foot against a stone" (RSV). But it is much more often the case that the opposite occurs—that a translation conveys only a faint whisper of the impact that is present in the original.

4. Connotation

This component is related to the quality of forcefulness just mentioned, but it focuses more specifically on the feelings, sentiments, and emotions which are communicated in the biblical discourse, especially by the speakers of the various dialogues. At times a CS which closely matches an expressive term of the SL text is available, e.g., *Kalanga ine*, roughly, "May I be punished!" (Chewa) for "Alas" (2 Kg 3.10). Or when the Psalmist exclaims, "Many *bulls* encompass me . . ." (22.12), most Tonga farmers cannot understand why he is so upset—to own so many bulls would, in fact, be quite a blessing! But when the formally similar "water buffalo" (*munyati*) is substituted, he gets the picture, for this beast is regarded as being very dangerous and unpredictable, as many an unwary hunter has learned to his hurt. Job's bitter expression of alienation, "My breath is offensive to my wife" (19.17), is not too different from the way the Mutonga would put it: "I stink to my wife" (i.e., as far as she is concerned), and that is the same as being cursed by her.

It is more common, however, to find that the CS diverges rather markedly from the literal form of the original. The suffering Psalmist may "*flood* his bed with tears" (6.6), but a Mutonga in the same emotional state would "*eat* his tears." The concept of "soul" which is often employed in Hebrew utterances that manifest deep feeling, e.g., "My *soul* also is sorely troubled" (6.3), must be replaced by "heart" in most Central African Bantu languages. Job complains that God throws him into a "slime pit" in Hebrew (9.31), but this becomes a "rubbish dump" (*dzala*) in a Chewa village setting. The Lord's promise of "dew" in Zc 8.12 needs to be rendered as "rain" (*mvula*) in Zambia and Malawi where dew is an insignificant factor in local agriculture.

An LT, on the other hand, will usually erase the connotative overtones of the SL text, which therefore has to be restructured in a more culturally specific way, e.g., through the addition of an exclamation: "Shall this fellow come into my house?" (1 Sm 21.15) to "*Ha*! this fellow, how has he entered my house?" (Chewa - i.e., to stress the disgust of the speaker); or by various syntactic and lexical shifts: "This is blood . . ." (2 Kg 3.23) to *Tee, mbulowa oobu*! 'Isn't it so, it's blood this!' (Tonga - i.e., to convey the amazement mixed with anticipation of the Moabite soldiers). An LT may even result in a skewing of emotive components in the RL, as for example, when David is described as having "beautiful eyes" (1 Sm 16.12), a characteristic which in most Central African languages is attributed only to attractive woman. Yahweh's prophecy to David that he will "chasten" his son if he is disobedient (2 Sm 7.14) often comes out with the wrong connotation in a translation, i.e., "I will *beat* him" (cp. GNB: "punish"). A socially more appropriate, "I will *correct/discipline* him" (Tonga), resolves the problem. In Tonga there is a distinctly negative association attached to the idea of having one's "sins covered" (Ps 32.1). It is as if the sinner deliberately tried to hide them from the view of society (sort of like "cover-up" in English). God must "rub them out" (or "erase") them instead.

A "collocational clash" often results when words which do not normally occur together in a language are combined, as in a literal translation. It sounds rather strange to a Tonga receptor, for example, to hear that God "teaches . . . the beasts of the earth" (Jb 35.11). Most animals are considered to be pretty stupid, so where does that leave man, to whom they are compared in this verse? But just as important is the connotational clash which a CS frequently produces in a text, for these are equally as damaging to the overall meaning of the biblical message. For example, Yahweh's command not to "turn to mediums and wizards" (Lv 19.31), but rather to "put them to death" (20.27) seems quite unjust to the traditionally-oriented Tonga listener, for who could be more helpful to the community than "the entered ones" (i.e., possessed with spirits of divination) and "medicine men"? These individuals help people in time of trouble (e.g., sickness, protection from witches, etc.) and enable them to achieve their goals in life (i.e., through magical charms and potions).

Such contradictory associations are obviously foreign to the sense intended by the original message, and the difference in perspectives can probably be corrected only by means of a footnote. Sometimes a textual solution may be possible, such as: simple deletion (e.g., "he who is born *of woman*" (Jb 25.4) since specifying the mother without the father in Tonga implies that the child was illegitimate); the use of a direct statement of the intended meaning in place of a figure of speech (e.g., "my mighty savior" instead of "horn of my salvation" (2 Sm 22.3) since "(animal) horn" (*nyanga*/Chewa) is often associated with various beliefs in witchcraft and sorcery); a more generic term (e.g., *mulema* (Tonga) "crippled person" instead of ". . . lame, or one who has a mutilated face or a limb too long . . ." (Lv 21.18) because the latter detailed description sounds frivolous or even impolite/rude); or a euphemism (e.g., replacing overt mention of "intercourse with your mother" (Lv 18.7, GNB), which is too shameful even to speak about, is this culturally oblique reference from Tonga: "do not enter your father's hut" and later in the verse, "do not approach her with respect to the body"). The translator must always be on guard against unwanted implications and associations slipping through unnoticed in his text, for these can be dangerous in more ways than one—for example, Christ's prediction that "the ruler of this world" will be "cast out" (Jn 12.31) must not be translated so as to allow for a possible reference to the current head of state!

5. *Naturalness*

This component applies to the social and stylistic aspects of discourse, in particular, those culturally specific expressions which are necessary to preserve authenticity and realism in direct speech. According to the Chewa conventions of deference, for example, it would not be possible for Abraham to say to the stranger who came to visit him at Mamre, "My lord, if I have found favor in your sight . . ." (Gn 18.3), for that would be placing his guest in a compromising position. It is the obligation of the host to "show favor" to his guests, not the reverse, as a literal translation would seem to suggest. Thus, a culturally more appropriate rendering would be: "Please, stay a while . . ."—that is, allow me the opportunity of serving you. When Eli the priest scolds Hannah for her apparent drunken behavior (1 Sm 1.14), a literal rendering is not only unnatural, but it also gives the wrong impression of his attitude towards her, i.e., he insults her. Thus, instead of: "Put away your wine from you," the Tonga says: "Go and become sober (lit. 'undrunk')" (i.e., in a single word: *Ukakololokwe*, which leaves the problematic term "wine" implicit).

The factors of role relations between speakers and levels of formality in the setting of speech, must also be kept in mind and applied to the present sociolinguistic situation as indicated by the original text. This will normally result in alterations being made in the form of direct discourse, e.g., to introduce a piece of advice given to a superior—instead of Naaman's maidservant appealing: "My father, if the prophet . . ." (2 Kg 5.13), she would say in Chewa: "Sorry, chief, but if the prophet . . ." Similarly, when addressing his master, the prophet Elisha, Gehazi would have shifted from a depreciatory self-reference to an honorific form of address: "your servant" (Hebrew) to "(my) master" (Chewa, 2 Kg 5.25). In rare instances, direct discourse may have to be converted into an indirect mode, e.g., in 2 Sm 1.26, where direct address is natural enough, but it would imply that David is speaking to Jonathan's "spirit."

One's concern for stylistic appropriateness, or a proper social register, in the translation must also take into consideration the nature of the Bible as a piece of sacred literature. Certain expressions, due to their associations with secular genres, both oral and written, may therefore sound out of place if employed in the Scriptures, e.g., "Hell is licking its chops" (Is 5.14, LB) for "Sheol has enlarged its appetite" (RSV).

It is often helpful to have some idea of the actual wording of the original (e.g., via a very literal or interlinear translation), for a modern version such as one in English may blur or even obliterate a natural correspondence that exists between the biblical and Bantu social perspectives and customs. In an instance of the converse of the preceding example, GNB has Eliphaz address Job directly in Jb 15.1—"Empty words, Job!"—whereas in a personal argument like this, the Tonga would prefer an indirect reference, as in the Hebrew: "Should a *wise man* answer with windy knowledge?" (RSV). The reason given by Lot's daughters for having an incestuous relation with their father is this: ". . . so that we may preserve offspring through our father" (Gn 19.32), which GNB changes to: ". . . so that we can have children." The original concern for perpetuating the clan has thus been turned into a motive that sounds too personal, or even selfish, from an African point of view. In any communal society, the needs of the individual must normally be subordinated to the interests of the group as a whole. In Ps 35.25, GNB renders the gloating of the ungodly as: "We are rid of him!" Literally, however, the text reads: "We have swallowed him up!" (RSV)—an expression that immediately suggested to the Tonga translators a natural equivalent: *Twamucha* 'We've trapped him!' (i.e., finished him off).

Occasionally, the translator will encounter instances of a violation in naturalness and appropriateness that cannot be rectified textually. If God had been a Mutonga, for example, he would surely have respected Adam's desire not to discuss business while the latter was "indecent" (i.e., naked) (Gn 3.10-11); he would have said something like, "All right, I'll come by again later on." In the biblical viewpoint, of course, Adam's perception of his nakedness was symptomatic of a far more serious problem that had developed in their relationship.

Our discussion of the three preceding factors (impact, connotation, and naturalness) would indicate that a cultural substitute is frequently necessary in order to achieve functional equivalence and versimilitude in the communication of the biblical message in the RL. Unfortunately, however, such equivalence cannot always be realized without suffering a certain loss with regard to other aspects of the message. The next three components involve semantic features of the original text which, in addition to that of form, are most commonly denied or distorted, at least to some extent, through the use of expressions of a culturally-specific nature. Though we will be focusing in this section upon the effect of a CS upon the accuracy and acceptability of a translation, it should be noted that some of the dangers presented here may also result wherever we have a literal translation of the SL text.

6. History

The historicity of the biblical texts constitutes one of the most important aspects of their authority and credibility. They were composed, under the inspiration of God, within a definite temporal and related sociocultural setting, and the meaning of their diverse messages cannot be completely, or even correctly, interpreted apart from that original context. Furthermore, a spiritual application of a given text to the contemporary scene cannot properly be made in isolation from the SL setting, since the latter must always serve as a norm that demarcates the limits and determines the direction of hermeneutical activity. The translator, then, will take the historical context seriously in his work and try to keep the distortion here (which is inevitable, considering the great span of time that has elapsed) to a minimum.

Such distortion, sometimes termed "anachronism," becomes the greatest when cultural substitutes are employed in the translation. The translator faces a real dilemma here: on the one hand, he wants to produce a "natural" text in his language—one that does not sound like a translation at all; yet on the other hand, he must respect the time-gap that is built into the message which he is trying to communicate. The principle here sounds simple enough: he must not twist or misrepresent the historical facts as set forth by the biblical text. But it is not always so easy to carry this out in practice and produce a translation that is really meaningful in the RL. We have already seen a number of examples of this, and more will be cited below.

When Christ, for example, likens himself to the "stone which . . . has become the head of the corner" (Mt 21.42), he is using an image (metaphor) that is at best unfamiliar to most people in Central Africa. Traditionally, houses were not built with stones, and even nowadays in towns they are constructed rather out of cement blocks or burnt bricks. A far more relevant comparison in this context, then, would be to the *mzati* 'centerpole' (Chewa) which supports the roof of a typical round, wattle, mud, and grass-thatched dwelling. The problem with such a proposal is, of course, that this was not the way in which houses were constructed in Palestine—at any time during the period of biblical history. The use of "centerpole" therefore misrepresents the historical (and cultural) setting. A nonliteral reference is involved in the original (according to the framework for evaluation proposed earlier), but there is a distinct temporal element present (since this is a prophetic text), and there is also a certain emphasis upon the component of form because this type of "house" is employed on other occasions with special religious significance (e.g., Ac 4.11). Another important consideration here is that a more literal translation, if modified (i.e., "the stone at the corner, *the most important one*"), though somewhat strange-sounding, can nevertheless be correctly understood, at least the potential is there, with some degree of probability.

The outright contradiction of an actual event in biblical history cannot really be considered as a translational option at all, e.g., to have Rebekah command Jacob to go and get two "chickens," instead of "kids" (chickens being much more frequently used for a special meal in contemporary Chewa culture), to prepare for Isaac (Gn 27.9). The same is true in direct speech; the substance of one's words cannot be altered in the interests of cultural relevance, as for example, when Elijah predicts that the food of the Tishbite widow will not fail "until the day that the LORD sends rain upon the earth" (1 Kg 17.14). That is a curious "blessing" from a Central African perspective since the food supply is normally the most deficient at that time of the year and it remains so until the first green crops can be harvested.

One must also observe that the form and function of a particular CS may indeed be similar to those of the original term, but the historical associations might be rather different, e.g., in the use of the Chewa *thangata* for "forced labor" (Gn 49.15); "impressed labor" to build roads, bridges, dams, etc. was practiced in colonial times (still within memory of many people) as a means of taxing those who had no money. Instances of anachronism in the translation base text should also be noted so that it is not reproduced in the RL, e.g., (from the Living Bible): "Tubal-cain . . . opened the first *foundry* (Gn 4.22); "Meanwhile the *crime rate* was rising rapidly across the earth . . ." (Gn 6.11); "These, then, were the descendants of Shem, classified according to their *political groupings* . . ." (Gn 10.31); "their children will not be born to be *cannon* fodder" (Is 65.23); "Nineveh was a very large city, *with extensive suburbs*" (Jo 3.3).

7. *Lifestyle*

This component encompasses the customs, traditions, and general way of life and behavior of a particular ethnic group. Under this category we are focusing upon the outward behavioral features of culture; the conceptual component will be treated in the next section. Problems relating to this aspect of the message are many and varied. Several examples will serve to illustrate some of this diversity as well as the importance of keeping the sociocultural component—both SL and RL—continually in focus during the translation process.

As we have seen, the SL culture will always feature certain practices for which there is no equivalent in the RL social environment. A notable OT example is concubinage, that is, the keeping of "secondary" wives of inferior social and legal status in the community. This is simply not allowed among the groups in Central Africa which have traditionally allowed polygamous marriages. A distinction is sometimes made between the "senior" wife (i.e., the first to be married) and one or more "junior" ones; this may involve a few extra privileges, but nothing more. According to tribal law, they are all equals. The translation of "concubine" (e.g., 2 Sm 3.7) thus presents conceptual problems which only a hybrid term can hope to solve (e.g., "woman/wife on the side" (Chewa) as distinct from "woman to the side," i.e., a secret lover; "servantwife/woman" (Tonga) as distinct from either the junior or senior wives). The notion of "viginity" (e.g., Mt 1.23) is similar in that there is no indigenous term for it, perhaps since in the past it was simply taken for granted as being a part of marriages which were arranged between families rather than individuals (often from the time of birth). There are, on the other hand, a number of practices which are very much the same in form and rationale, such as the custom of levirate marriage, where in the event of a man's death, a close relative will be chosen to incorporate the widow into his own family unit (*kulya zina* 'to eat the name' in Tonga; *kulowa chokolo* 'to enter chokolo,' the latter referring in Chewa to a type of protective medicine eaten at the time of an adult's funeral).

When it comes to the use of a cultural substitute, however, one must carefully investigate to see exactly how the respective practices differ. Any significant skewing of the biblical way of doing things must be avoided if at all possible, e.g., in reference to a woman who was bought as a slave (Ex 21.8), it would not be correct to say: "(her master) must allow her to leave, *without being paid back the bridewealth*," for the latter would imply to Tonga receptors that a socially-sanctioned marriage had been established. Similarly, one would not be justified in altering the command: "thou shalt rise up before the hoary head" (Lv 19.32) to the gesture of "kneeling" as would be customary in a Chewa context—or to substitute "drum" for a "lyre" when translating the advice given to Saul to help him get rid of the "evil spirit" that was troubling him (1 Sm 16.16, since musical therapy featuring drumming is commonly used for this purpose among the peoples of Central Africa.

All of the preceding involved literal, legal or historical texts where fidelity to the outward form of the procedure or object is much more important. Even in nonhistorical or poetic texts, such as the prophetic books, care must be taken not to replace references to actual cultural practices with substitutes from an alien social environment, e.g., "Divine Truth comes to them through *tea leaves*" (Ho 4.12, LB), whereas the original probably had reference to rabdomancy, a method of divining through the use of special wooden rods.

8. World-View

This component complements the behavioral aspect of a people's culture which was considered above. It refers to the "world-view," that is, their beliefs, values, presuppositions, norms, etc., upon which all of their external activity, both word and deed, is based. To be sure, it is at times a rather arbitrary exercise to attempt to distinguish which factor is in focus when discussing a particular problem of translational equivalence. Nevertheless, the "psychological setting" is mentioned here primarily to assert its importance and to ensure that it is not overlooked in the process of analysis, since differences between source and receptor cultures in this regard are not always so obvious.

The translator must learn to reckon with this component of meaning even in the case of a literal rendering. A local folk belief ("superstition") or custom may be called to mind, or reinforced, by what seem to be the most innocuous passages. The statement that "Saul eyed David from that day on" (1 Sm 18.9), for example, would tend to suggest to many receptors in Central Africa that Saul was a witch, clearly bent upon destroying his supposed rival to the throne. This assumption is immediately confirmed in the text by Saul's attempt to "pin David to the wall" with his spear (18.10-11). The report that "doctors applied medicine" (i.e., embalmed) Jacob's body (Gn 50.2) could only mean that this was being done to protect it from being removed from the grave and eaten by witches. Often, of course, the difficulty is increased whenever a figure of speech is involved. The reference to one's "tent-cord" being "plucked up" (Jb 4.21) would appear on the surface to correspond to Tonga funerary practice, for a married person's house is normally destroyed or simply left to rot when he (or she) dies in order to prevent the return of the spirit of the deceased.

Situations, objects, and events that correspond formally between SL and RL may well differ in significance due to the differing cultural perspectives of the people. Hezekiah's "boil" (2 Kg 20.7), for example, certainly does not sound life-threatening to most receptors in Central Africa, for these are a common, and not too serious, occurrence. Hezekiah, it seems, is making a big thing out of what was really rather insignificant. The action of the Roman soldiers at the time of Jesus's crucifixion is also a source of considerable misunderstanding: how could they presume to take the clothes of a perfect stranger and proceed to apportion them at the time of his death (Jn 19.23-24)? In a traditional context, this would be done only by the closest relatives of the deceased. Surely, according to popular belief, the persons who "won" the coat would lose out in the end by being plagued by Jesus' vengeful spirit!

The preceding examples demonstrate that a literal translation by no means guarantees the exclusion of misleading associations. It is probably true to say, however, that the use of a cultural substitute does make the message somewhat more prone to this type of conceptual perversion. For example, use of the Tonga verb *vumununa* 'to cover over (as with a cloth)' for "strike with blindness" in 2 Kg 6.18 would suggest that Elisha is indeed a powerful "medicine man," for this is exactly what the latter would do in such a dangerous situation (i.e., to afflict his foes with a special perceptual "blindness" through the use of special charms), and his protective action would be referred to by the very same word. Similarly, to employ the idiomatic expression "Did I swallow a stone" (Tonga) for "Is my strength the strength of stones" (Jb 6.12, answer "no" implied) involves a very subtle difference in perception. On the surface, the meaning is the same, i.e., "Do I have the power to prolong my life?"—but on a deeper level of significance we find that the Tonga question conveys some unwanted implications, namely: I did not obtain medicine from the herbalist in order to protect my heart (together with my "spirit name") from witches/sorcerers by magically sealing it inside a special stone.

Translators normally have problems with the Hebrew word "Sheol" since it has several different senses according to the context. And in Central Africa, at least, the solution does not seem to lie in the use of a CS, e.g., "In the place of ghosts (*kubusangu*) who is able to praise you?" (Tonga), for such a rendering would overtly suggest that the Hebrews had exactly the same traditional belief concerning the ancestral spirits as the Bantu. These examples indicate that due to the pervasive nature of religion as an element of African culture, the religious component of their world-view is of particular importance to translators. Indeed, the aspect of meaning is of extra significance due to the very nature of the Bible as a theological text, and therefore it needs to be given special attention in the communication process.

A brief consideration of demon possession as encountered in the New Testament might serve to illustrate this point further. There are three basic ways of handling a text such as, "he has a demon" (Jn 10.20). Use of a loanword, in Tonga at least—i.e., *daimona* (as in the old Bible)—conveys both a denotation and a connotation which is very different from that intended by the original. Certain people, especially women, welcome "entrance" by such a demon-spirit, which is frequently said to be the ancestral spirit of some well-known biblical personage. This is because the spirit enables the possessed person, once a trance has been induced, to be employed in the practice of divination, and hence to earn a living. Secondly, the use of a cultural substitute, i.e., *sikazwa* 'malevolent ancestral spirit,' while preserving the negative associations of the original, distort its semantic content in that the "demons" of Bible times were considered to be of nonhuman, Satanic origin. The only solution left was to employ a generic word plus modifier, viz. *muuya mubi*, lit. 'bad breath,' which besides having a rather different meaning within the traditional Tonga ontological system, i.e., "evil disposition," in some respects sounds more appropriate for use in a modern toothpaste commercial!

The Mosaic ritual of atonement illustrates the problem which we have observed on a number of occasions where a cultural substitute—which in this case is very close to the literal equivalent—involves a whole complex of events and objects, rather than just a single referent. As stipulated in Lv 16.10, a "scapegoat," after the appropriate preliminary ceremony which included the sacrifice of another goat, was driven out into the wilderness bearing "all the iniquities of the people of Israel" (v. 21). Two crucial religious components are present: there is a sacrifical death which signifies life for the people, and there is a ritual separation symbolizing the removal of sins. These same two elements are emphasized in the corresponding Tonga practice, which is intended to rid the community of a marauding lion (or similar beast). This lion is believed to have been sent by the ancestral spirits who are offended because of the current lack of religious devotion on the part of the people. They therefore need "something to eat." At the climax of the ritual for appeasing these spirits, a black cow is taken out to the burial ground or to a local rain shrine, and after a number of prayers pleading forgiveness and requesting acceptance, the cow is left with the words, "Here is your meat." If all goes according to plan, the lion will return that night, feast on the sacrificial cow, and will then leave the area as a sign that the spirits have forgiven "their children."

For a more abstract theological concept, consider Paul's expression, "our old self" (lit. "man") (Ro 6.6), meaning one's total unregenerate being as opposed to the spiritually new personality made possible through Christ. In many languages, a literal translation might easily give the impression that one's grandfather is being referred to, were it not for the fact a crucifixion is involved. Contrived terms have the problem of remaining distinct from the expression "sinful body," i.e., human nature and its physical attributes as controlled by sin, which also occurs in this verse. To solve this difficulty, the Tonga coined an abstract term which is based upon the pejorative designation *muntunsi* 'person of the land,' that is to say, someone who has no spiritual values (in a traditional sense) and is concerned only about himself. He does not bother about paying homage to the ancestors and is therefore a danger to the community at large should the former decide to seek retribution. Such an anti-social person (in the broader, religious sense) is commonly thought to be eventually punished with insanity. "Person-of-the-land-ness" is thus a relatively familiar religious idea and does have several components in common with those of the original term. There are, on the other hand, a few alien features—in particular, the connection with the immediate spirit world and the socially-oriented nature of the offense—and so the translator can only try the term out to see which components win out from the perspective of his receptors' understanding. It might be noted in this connection that the more esoteric, dualistic Greco-Roman worldview which colors certain key sections of the Pauline epistles is particularly difficult to render meaningfully in a Bantu context due to the great difference in perspective that is involved, e.g., the contrast between "mind/spirit" and "body/flesh," "law of God" and "law of sin," "life" and "death" or "good" and "evil" coexisting within a person as expounded in Romans 7.

The religious associations of an expression are also important on the extratextual level of communication. Prominent members of the receptor constituency may object to the use of a given word on account of its links with the past, namely, its "involvement" within the traditional worship system. Such terminology is often viewed as being implicitly supportive of ancient, non-Christian beliefs and is thus viewed with suspicion, or even strong opposition. The report that Joseph's servant, for example, distinguished his master's missing cup with the words, ". . . by this cup he divines" (Gn 44.5), has caused a problem for certain church leaders among the Chewa. "We are preaching against the rituals of divination," they protested, "and to allow a Christian [*sic*] like Joseph to practice it (as implied by using the CS *ombeza*) would hurt our message!"

Any translational solution, from the most literal correspondence to the freest type of cultural substitute, may be evaluated with respect to these eight semantic features and then compared with any other available option in the RL. The results would then have to be related to a similar componential profile of the SL expression under consideration. As has been suggested, both the textual as well as the extratextual contexts need to be taken into account in order to get a more complete picture of the different factors of form, function, association, and usage involved. The goal, as always, is to determine in the RL the closest, natural communication equivalent of the SL message. As further illustration of this process of evaluation—of weighing the pros and cons of the different possibilities—two more complicated examples are discussed below.

The term *baamaah* 'high places' presents a typical set of translational problems and possibilities in most Bantu languages, for instance, in a passage like: "I (the LORD) will destroy your high places" (Lv 26.30). Originally this word probably referred to shrines dedicated to Canaanite deities which were actually erected at places of greater than normal elevation, "on every high hill" (1 Kg 14.23). In later usage, however, the term seems to have been extended to include all such shrines, no matter where they might occur (e.g., 2 Kg 23.8, 1 Ch 16.39, Jr 7.31). The religious ritual conducted at these high places involved animal sacrifices to the deity (1 Kg 3.2) and were often associated with the symbols of Baal and Asherah, namely, "pillars and Asherim" (Ex 34.12f, 1 Kg 14.23). The purpose of such rites was to ensure the fertility of the land, in all of its aspects, and so they were normally connected with grossly immoral practices on the part of the devotees, thus compounding the sin of idolatry (Ho 4.12-14).

Now a literal translation of this term in a language like Tonga, viz. *masena aakujulu* 'the places up above,' is either meaningless or misleading, i.e., the phrase could be misunderstood as a some sort of poetic reference to *kujulu* 'heaven.' A descriptive expression is stylistically awkward, i.e., "a place for sacrificing to images in the hills" (Tonga) and could also be misleading since "images" were not part of the indigenous worship practice. The local equivalent to a "high place" in the Tonga religious system is the *maleende* shrine. These are not usually found in the hills, but then, as was suggested above, the component of high elevation was not always, or even usually, prominent in OT usage. A *maleende* is widely regarded as being a place where certain ancestral spirits (*basangu*) congregate and therefore where they can be consulted in times of trouble, notably a period of drought. Some extraordinary natural object often marks the spot, e.g., an unusual-looking tree or rock, and sometimes the grave of some important personage is located there, e.g., a "rainmaking" priest. These features also seem to have been connected with the biblical high places, as were the shelters which were often constructed there (1 Kg 12.31; in Tonga: *twaanda twamaleende* 'little houses/huts of the rain shrine').

Apart from these apparent componential similarities (i.e., formal, dynamic, cultural, theological), there are also some important contrasts. Chief among these would be the more specific religious function of the Tonga shrines (i.e., from general fertility narrowed to primarily rainmaking and other problem-solving purposes, such as disease), together with the somewhat different direct beneficiary, i.e., "god" versus the ancestral spirits (although the Tonga do believe that these spirits function as intermediaries between the living and Leza). There is also a certain degree of historical distortion, or anachronism, involved, since the use of *maleende* would imply that the Hebrews were observing the same or similar religious rites as the Tonga. There is, however, a strong connotative factor within the current RL setting which would support the use of this cultural equivalent, for just as the prophets of old, so also God's servants today must warn against the danger of a widespread syncretistic tendency which continually seeks to incorporate the beliefs and practices of traditional, pre-Christian forms of worship.

The second example is taken from the NT and centers on the issue of employing cultural substitutes in figurative language. The passage concerned is Christ's warning to his disciples as recorded in Mt 10.16:

"Behold, I send you out as *sheep* in the midst of *wolves*; so be as wise as *serpents* and innocent as *doves*.

"A back translation of the Tonga (draft) reads as follows:

"Look, I am sending you out as *sheep* among *wild dogs*. Therefore, you must be as clever as *partridges* and as gentle as *pigeons*."

Upon evaluating this translation, we encounter a conflict in communication priorities, since no single solution can claim complete equivalence, that is, in all functional aspects of the message. A literal rendering of the Greek can be made quite easily in Tonga. It would thus be possible to remain relatively close to the formal and semantic features of the original (some noteworthy divergences are pointed out below). However, such formal correspondence causes rather serious difficulties with regard to some of the other components which we have discussed, those pertaining to connotation and world-view in particular. These problems arise because the associative qualities which are attached to the respective referents by Tonga receptors do not match. For this reason, a strict transference of the denotative content of the figures must be reconsidered in the light of what they will actually mean in the current RL context of communication and what effect this will have upon today's readers.

In this connection it is necessary to examine the sociocultural context in which this text is to be realized. It is not possible to ignore the positive or negative associations which Tonga speakers place upon the various translational alternatives. The fact that this is only the second translation of the Bible for a relatively uneducated (with regard to religious knowledge), nonliterate (i.e., under 50%), and unsophisticated (i.e., in the use of literary aids such as footnotes, etc.)

constituency would tend to lead one along the path of a greater degree of cultural adaptation in the renderings proposed. In this case, a translation which emphasizes "naturalness" a bit more than "closeness" happens to approximate the formal component on the generic level in that the result sounds more like didactic "wisdom lore" (e.g., proverbs, riddles, etc.) which comprise an important part of the Tonga oral tradition. There is thus a harmony of form, content, function, and association which a literal reproduction cannot achieve. The notes below explain the rationale behind some of the major decisions that were made in working toward a dynamic equivalent representation of the Greek in Chitonga.

mbelele 'sheep'

Despite the fact that *mpongo* 'goats' are far more common among indigenous Tonga farmers (sheep being restricted for the most part to large commercial ranches, often those operated by Europeans) and that sheep are associated more with stupidity rather than helplessness and meekness as in the original, the literal reference to sheep is retained, since the people at least know of them. Furthermore, goats are generally regarded as being rather cautious animals, for they rarely venture very far from their stockade and quickly rush for shelter even when it begins to rain. A goat would be far less likely to get caught by a "wolf" than a sheep, a fact which would tend to blunt the point of the comparison. There is also the importance of sheep as a symbolic word with considerable religious significance in the Bible (e.g., sheep and goats at the Last Judgment, the Good Shepherd, the Lamb of God, etc.), and this would strongly favor preserving the reference if at all possible.

baumpe 'wild dogs'

The source text's "wolves" are unknown in Central Africa, so one is forced to look for the nearest equivalent. The problem is that there are two possibilities, each of which possesses some, but not all, of the characteristics of the Palestinian wolf. *Basuntwe* 'hyenas' hunt at night and are the principal predators of livestock in rural areas. They are traditionally depicted as greedy creatures, but also as sneaky cowards. "Wild dogs" are crafty, relentless hunters, but they tend to attack mainly during the day and in packs (unlike the biblical wolf). They also stick to the remoter regions of the land where they have less contact with man and his livestock. However, they are noted for their cruelty and fierceness, and since this appears to be the component in focus in this comparison, wild dogs, rather than hyenas, was chosen in the translation.

kwale 'partridges'

Here is a case where a literal translation would cause a serious collocational clash in the mind of the Tonga reader due to the explicit mention of the ground of comparison, i.e., "wise." The snake is only too familiar to all Batonga, but experience and tradition has led them to identify it as the epitome, not of wisdom, but of malicious jealousy: the snake bites and even kills, not for food like the other animals, but apparently out of pure spite and treachery. This is definitely not the quality that Christ meant to attribute to his disciples here. The negative associations connected with snakes in the local receptor environment would be automatically applied to the referent in the text, thus provoking a serious connotative contradiction (i.e., the disciples are assumed to be positive.)

The partridge is obviously not a close equivalent in form, but functionally it is the most natural substitute, especially since the figure is being used as a teaching device (i.e., nonliteral, ahistorical, focus on impact). The Batonga consider partridges to be clever birds because they only rarely get trapped, and if one does happen to get caught, other partridges, it is said, will always avoid that particular spot in the future. Additional support for this choice is derived from the contextual setting of the Bible itself. This bird was well known in Palestine, and there are indications that it, too, may have been figuratively associated with cleverness and cautiousness (cf. Jr 17.11). While physically the partridge is rather far removed from a snake, it is, on the other hand, very similar to the "dove" in Christ's second descriptive attribution.

Sulwe 'hare,' the embodiment of slyness and craft in Tonga traditional lore, could not be used due to the high degree of culturizing (i.e., distortion in favor of the receptor culture) which this would introduce into the message. This "trickster" character of folktale fame is just too well known and stereotyped to fit the biblical context. In addition, "hare" is unsuitable, because, as an essentially amoral personage, he is also linked with the attribute of deceit and is frequently cast in the role of the cultural antitype—one who flaunts his nonconformity to the ancient values and mores of society.

nkwilimba 'pigeons'

This figurative designation is the closest in both form and function to the original. However, there is a slight problem of specification in that the Tonga makes a distinction between wild and domesticated doves/pigeons, whereas the Greek does not. According to popular belief, the wild variety, *nziba* 'doves', are not characterized by their gentleness (or "innocence"), but their domestic relatives definitely are. It is widely held that pigeons can be raised only by persons with matching dispositions, namely, kind and gentle. However, if the opposite type of individual tries to raise them, they will all soon fly away.

The preceding examples suggest how the many facets of receptor culture impinge upon the general considerations of form and function to complicate the process of finding the closest natural equivalent of the biblical text. As we have seen, it is virtually impossible to adequately close all of the communication gaps that appear in the transfer of the message from one historical and cultural setting to another. The aim is simply to eliminate as many of the points of potential misunderstanding as possible. The translator, however, will not always be able to achieve even this minimal goal. He will on occasion have to deal with passages involving conceptual problems which defy all attempts at textual solution—where only some type of extratextual aid must be sought. A few of these are illustrated below.

Some cultural contradictions between the biblical and Bantu peoples are occasioned by a simple difference in customs, in their characteristic ways of doing things. God's command not to "eat any blood whatever" (Lv 7.26) sounds most extreme to the cattle-loving Tonga people who consider cooked blood (mixed with "fat" which is prohibited in 7.23) to be a special delicacy.

Most problems arise, however, due to a contrast in their underlying world-view, their respective belief systems, which of course concern every aspect of life from birth to death. In Ho 13.13, for example, the people of Israel are likened to a rebellious child which is so stubborn that it refuses even to be born. If a Tonga child's delivery does not go smoothly, however, it is considered to be the mother's fault: either the child is the product of an adulterous relation (and she must confess who the real father is before the birth can take place), or she is a foolish woman for having started to "push" too soon, that is, while the baby was still "sleeping" inside the womb. When the son of the widow of Zarephath suddenly dies, the woman accuses Elijah of being the "witch" who caused the death (1 Kg 17.18). At least that is how the story could well be interpreted in a Tonga sociocultural context, for the pattern of events seems to suggest this: there is the unexplained nature of the death coupled with the presence of Elijah, the mysterious and obviously powerful stranger who has come to live in the very same house. The woman's accusation is phrased rather indirectly, but the implication is clear. Her suspicions are confirmed by the fact that Elijah says nothing in his defense, but having been exposed as the culprit, he immediately attempts to set things right again through his magical powers (the only difference being that a suspected witch would never be left alone to effect a "cure" upon his victim, v. 19).

Similarly, conceptual "interference" tends to blur the point of Christ's parable of the woman with seven husbands (Mt 22.25-28). For the average Tonga receptor the crucial issue has nothing to do with whose wife the woman would be in heaven (or whether there is a resurrection at all), but why was she not properly "cleansed" (through ritual sexual intercourse) to prevent all these deaths from happening—or how could those men be so stupid as to agree to marry such a dangerous "uncleansed woman" (i.e., one who was not freed from the lingering jealous spirit of the first deceased husband)? For the Mutonga, the important question concerns the social implications of this case here and now—not its possible relevance to the dim thereafter.

Then there are those crucial theological terms which cannot approach in translation the significance that they possess in the original. Such incongruence may be due to the foreignness of the concept involved for which there may not be any suitable RL equivalent (e.g., the notions of a future place/state of punishment or blessing in "hell"/"heaven"), or it may arise on account of the limitations of linguistic form to capture the essence of the biblical expression. An example of the latter is the prophetic epithet that Christ applied to himself—the "Son of Man" (e.g., Jn 5.27). In most Central African languages, a literal rendering of this phrase (which is the only one that has been acceptable to the churches) means, in a nonreligious context, *Mwanaamuntu* 'somebody's child' (Tonga). Not only is the expression vague, it is also somewhat pejorative, for every legitimate child must have parents who are known in the community. In a more specific secular context, the term could even mean "the child of an African," for in contrast to a European whose conceptual classification is (or was, originally) unclear, an African is definitely a *muntu* 'person'!

The suitability, or acceptability, of such attempts at equivalence—the apparent successes as well as the obvious failures—need to be thoroughly tested before a translation is fixed in print. This testing should incorporate both oral and written procedures for determining the degree of accuracy, intelligibility, readability, and naturalness of the terms that have been proposed. A functionally-oriented communication model can serve as a useful framework for such an exercise, especially if it is employed in conjunction with the practice of drawing up a componential profile to focus more precisely upon the different areas of similarity and contrast which are manifested by the respective sets of SL and RL terms. A broad cross section of the receptor constituency must be included in such a testing program (for a more detailed presentation of this topic, see "Training Translators About Style" in *The Bible Translator*, Jan., 1982). In cases where one is not able to clear up the points of possible misunderstanding within the text itself (by means of the various procedures which have been discussed above), then one will have to do this extratextually, e.g., through footnotes, a glossary of key terms, section headings, cross references, illustrations, tables, maps, an index, book introductions, and so forth. One thing needs to be emphasized in suggesting these different devices: the translator cannot assume that a textual problem (whether of form or function, linguistic or cultural) can be eliminated simply because it has been dealt with somewhere outside of the text proper. The receptor must still be taught *how* to use a footnote or glossary, for example, before such information becomes available to him—and with that the potential solution to his difficulty.

The importance of these various types of supplementary aid cannot be overestimated: anything which can help readers to understand the biblical message more completely and correctly will increase the practical value of a translation, and hence its acceptability among the receptor constituency. This is particularly true in the case of a new translation, which is the current situation for many of the major languages of Central and Southern Africa. The great majority of the older versions of this region were published without note or comment of any kind, except possibly for cross references and larger section headings. This new generation of Bible translation needs to extend its concern for meaning—for idiomaticity as well as intelligibility—beyond the text itself so that receptors can participate much more fully in the communication process whereby the seed of the Word is sown and takes root in the soil of a new linguistic and cultural setting.

Books referred to:

Louw J. P., ed. 1985. *Lexicography and Translation*. Bible Society, Cape Town.

Nida E. A. 1975. *Componential Analysis of Meaning*. Mouton, The Hague.

Wendland E. R. 1985. *Language, Society and Bible Translation*. Bible Society, Cape Town.

Chapter 3

Tackling an Old Testament Text (Genesis 15)

Théo R. Schneider

1. Translating aloud

Regional workshops for Bible translators offer a number of obvious advantages. Participants have time to experiment with oral procedures in the rendering of selected texts. Various teams working on cognate languages within a similar sociocultural context can easily be grouped and begin to interact in daily translation assignments. They may discover lexical and stylistic affinities or contrasts between their respective vernaculars. They can exchange useful ideas for the translation of the same source material. They can warn each other against unnecessary interference, either by the form of the biblical base or by its so-called "model" version in Western languages. These points, expanded below, form the conclusion of the present chapter, which aims at describing a translation workshop experience on the text of Genesis 15.

The first advantage of putting several translation teams to work on a common passage such as Genesis 15 is to expose the members of each team to various oral possibilities in the treatment of the selected chapter from the Old Testament. Its Hebrew text will have been presented and analysed in a plenary session during the morning. The afternoon is spent in various tentative reconstructions of the pericope in each of the receptor languages represented at the workshop. At each step of the exercise, members of an individual team normally start by discussing the biblical material and then share several possible renderings of its words and phrases. In this type of preliminary oral interaction the Hebrew text is first being translated aloud. Its lexical units, grammatical constructions, and rhetorical features must first pass the test of an acceptable "re-telling" before being committed to writing. In other words, the translators must first listen to each other and "hear" the text which they are about to draft. This is the best way for them to approach its reconstruction, in view of its prospective hearers and readers within the receptor constituency.

The second advantage of a regional translation workshop consists in bringing together in the same room two or three teams working on neighboring projects within a comparable cultural environment. The team members can then interact orally, share drafting suggestions, and deal together with similar problems of functional equivalence in the rendering of the Hebrew base. Allowance must be made at this stage for the inevitable semantic and rhetorical peculiarities of each language represented on the translation panel.

The third positive result of a combined translation exercise is to guard against a mere imitation of the usual Western models such as RSV, NIV, GNB, NEB, NAV, BFC or BHD.[1] Related African languages, for instance, may discover that for a natural rendering of the biblical message they have much more in common than anything they might have noticed in the Western versions. In the course of their discussion the translators within a certain language zone are able to take stock of their stylistic resources for the translation of a particular literary genre. They should feel free to borrow from each other out of a similar store of denotative or associative meanings in order to render the same Hebrew lexical units. In the translation process they may share figures of speech or idioms which are totally absent from the model versions, but which occur in their own range of rhetorical features.

Each cooperating team is then in a position to draft verse by verse its rendering of the selected passage, and to add an English interlinear back-translation. The team should also be encouraged to draw up a list of linguistic or contextual problems encountered in the course of the practical session. In order to complete the procedure, some of the basic issues raised during the drafting periods should be summarized and reviewed the following day at the beginning of the next plenary session.

A few additional indications on method and presuppositions may be appropriate at this stage. In our opinion, one of the conditions for successful teamwork during a Bible translation workshop consists in thorough exegetical preparation. Such an introduction to the text is normally given during the plenary session. Its perspective should be as scholarly and broad as possible. Problems regarding the integrity of the Masoretic text must be faced openly on the basis of the BHS apparatus or of the Hebrew Old Testament Text Project (HOTTP) report. Each textual variant, however, must still be assessed from the translator's special point of view, since not all such variants will prove significant for a meaningful rendering of the source message. For example, a well-attested discrepancy between the Masoretic text and ancient versions, such as the Septuagint or the Vulgate, may be due to legitimate translational adjustments in these versions, rather than to a different underlying Hebrew text.

---

[1] For a list of abbreviations, see p. 62.

In any case, an exegetical, and thereby theological, choice between various possible renderings of a difficult passage cannot be avoided, and an appropriate footnote may be required. Modern translators should not be guided by so-called model versions when making such a choice, because these may not exhibit a consensus in their textual options.

As a further preparatory step, an in-depth literary evaluation of the selected text is essential for translators. The aim is to bring the structure of the passage and its main or subsidiary themes into focus, with the help of commentaries, handbooks, and other specialized studies. These should give the translators some idea of the long history of oral tradition, composition, redaction, and transmission, which forms the background of the text to be translated. Such an understanding of the formation of a biblical passage through many centuries should help and encourage the modern Bible translators. After all, this is part of their own history, and they are adding their own chapter to the remarkable saga of the transmission of the biblical text. They should be proud of playing such a role, whatever their personal attitude might be regarding such problems as authorship, source hypotheses, form and transmission criticism and dating proposals.

Furthermore, the exegetical preparation should try to situate the selected text in its wider literary setting (perspective, code, specific tradition) and in its external context (sociohistorical situation). An inventory and analysis of its key-terms, grammatical constructions, and rhetorical features, as well as a discussion of the semantic relations between its nuclear phrases, will undoubtedly contribute to a more faithful and satisfactory translation process. In the end a translation may be proposed that will be really meaningful, especially in terms of avoiding, as far as possible, the possibility of misunderstanding on the part of the receptor.

2. Overview of the text

In the translation exercise described below, the aim had been to cover the Old Testament portion of Genesis 15.1-21 in one day. This proved too much for a team to tackle during one afternoon drafting session, and only verses 1 to 6 were dealt with. Nevertheless, the morning preparation had presented the whole chapter, and thus delineated the correct macro-level framework for the treatment of the first section 15.1-6.

The following contemporary versions furnish two different models for a possible reconstruction of the selected text. A simplified layout of Genesis 15.1-6, as close as possible to the Hebrew kernel phrases, is given below under paragraph 2.5 pp. 53-54. These pages also contain a description of the kind of semantic relations which give coherence to the narrative.

NIV: Genesis 15

God's covenant with Abram

1) After this, the word of the LORD came to Abram in a vision:
     "Do not be afraid, Abram.
     I am your shield,P your very great reward.q"
2) But Abram said, "O Sovereign LORD, what can you give me since I remain childless and the one who will inheritᵣ my estate is Eliezer of Damascus?"
3) And Abram said, "You have given me no children, so a servant in my household will be my heir."
4) Then the word of the LORD came to him: "This man will not be your heir, but a son coming from your own body will be your heir."
5) He took him outside and said, "Look at the heavens and count the stars—if indeed you can count them." Then he said to him, "So shall your offspring be."
6) Abram believed the LORD and he credited it to him as righteousness.

GNB: Genesis 15

God's covenant with Abram

1) After this, Abram had a vision and heard the LORD say to him, "Do not be afraid, Abram. I will shield you from danger and give you a great reward."
2) But Abraham answered, "Sovereign LORD, what good will your reward do me, since I have no children? My only heir is Eliezer of Damascus.ˣ
3) You have given me no children, and one of my slaves will inherit my property."
4) Then he heard the LORD speaking to him again: "This slave Eliezer will not inherit your property; your own son will be your heir."
5) The LORD took him outside and said, "Look at the sky and try to count the stars; you will have as many descendants as that."

6) Abram put his trust in the LORD, and because of this the LORD was pleased with him and accepted him.

P or "sovereign."
q or "shield/your reward will be very great."
ᵣ The meaning of the Hebrew for this phrase is uncertain.
ˣ "My . . . Damascus"; Hebrew unclear.

2.1 Paragraphing

When comparing model versions of Genesis 15 with the nearly compact Hebrew text of BHS, the first feature translators should notice is their wide difference in terms of number and location of paragraphs. Interestingly enough, these differences do not correspond with the usual classification of modern versions into "formal" versus "dynamic." The position is as follows:

Number of paragraphs	Initial verses
BHS : 3	1, 10, 16
RSV : 4	1, 7, 12, 17
NB : 9	1, 2, 4, 6, 7, 8, 9, 12, 17
NIV : 10	1, 2, 4, 6, 7, 8, 9, 10, 12, 17
NEB : 2	1, 6
NAV : 12	1, 2, 3, 4, 5, 6, 7, 8, 9, 10, 12, 17
TOB : 5	1, 3,7,12,19
BFC : 9	1, 2, 4, 5, 6, 9, 10, 12, 17
BHD : 8	1, 2, 4, 6, 7, 12, 14, 17

For a narrative text such as Genesis 15, the typographical device of paragraphing carries an important meaning and is functionally very significant. It should help the silent or public reader to receive an immediate visual perception of how the narrative proceeds. It should also indicate the logical sequence and the transitions of the story in its final canonical form, and it certainly affects performance.

One cannot escape the impression of arbitrariness in most of the above divisions. Paragraphing should be strictly controlled and should be introduced only where the real pauses or transitions occur in the narrative, namely, in this case at verses 7, 12 and 17 as explained below. Five out of eight of the consulted versions have in fact started a new paragraph at these three verses; they have thereby reflected the broad scholarly consensus regarding the composite nature of Genesis 15.

The workshop drafts were handwritten and do not, therefore, present any clear pattern in paragraphing, with the exception of the translation in Kwanyama, which opened a new paragraph at v. 5, like NAV and BFC, but arbitrarily added a section heading at that unlikely place. The other translation teams would, of course, be forced to organize their rendering of Genesis 15 into paragraphs at the typing stage, but the Western model versions would prove of very little help to them in that respect.

The only true guarantee and precondition for meaningful paragraphing reside in a clear understanding of the literary form of the text, based on redaction history, rhetorical data, subject matter, and discourse structure.

2.2 Verse divisions and combinations

Verse divisions and combinations should reflect the basic structural organization of a pericope. BFC and BHD have combined verses 2 and 3, thus hiding the fact that these two verses form a clear doublet. The Masoretic text betrays here a somewhat awkward editorial hand. GNB simply drops the repeated opening formula *wayyomer Abhram*. On the contrary, NAB starts a new paragraph at v. 3, but expands with a gloss *Abram het verder gesê* (Abram went on to say).

Should translators be encouraged to apply such cosmetic treatment on the often pock-marked face of the biblical text? Are they supposed to systematically sandpaper its rough edges? Basic theological attitudes are of course involved in such decisions. The least advice one could give to translators is *not* to try and improve at all cost a final, undisputed form of the Masoretic text, as presented by a standard edition such as BHS. Translators should combine verses or make use of square brackets with footnotes, only in cases of well-attested textual variants of that text.

Some of the workshop drafts, namely, those in Chewa, Herero, Kung, and Tonga have followed GNB and skipped the opening formula in v. 3. The Nama team has expanded like NAV with a conjunctive gloss: *!Arulîb ge (Abramma) ge mî* 'Further he (A) said.' Swati also linked v. 3 with v. 2 by saying *Abrama wachubeka watsi* 'Abram continued and said.' The Tsonga team simply rendered by *Abrama a tlhela a ku* 'Abram again said,' using an adverbial construction (derived from a verb) to express the consecutive *waw* at the beginning of v. 3 in Hebrew, along the lines of NAV.

The initial *waw* of v. 2 should be taken as semantically adversative. NIV and GNB have rendered it correctly by "but," followed by Chewa (*koma*), S. Ndebele (*kodwana*), Swati (*kodvwa*), and Venda (*huno*). Others, namely, Tsonga, Mbukushu, and Nama, have reconstructed the phrase as "Abram answered and said," thus somewhat obscuring the adversative meaning of *waw* in this context.

2.3 Headings and themes

When approaching a text, the next feature on which translators should focus their attention is its heading or its subheadings, as given in versions and commentaries. Ideally, a section heading should summarize the theme of the pericope at hand, using words and phrases from the text itself in the most compact manner. With their common heading "God's covenant with Abram" for Genesis 15, NIV and GNB have succeeded in being concise, but they have missed the central theme of the chapter, namely, God's promise to Abram, *not* primarily his covenant with the patriarch, as will be seen at the end of this sub-section. In fact, God's covenant with Abraham will form the main theme of Genesis 17, where the key term *berith* is used not less than thirteen times, while it is used only once in Genesis 15 (v. 18).

The usual procedure in a translation team is to start by rendering the heading of the day's passage and writing it neatly at the top of a fresh page. The standard list of headings published by the United Bible Societies, or a heading in one of the model versions can be trusted in this matter. The team should assume that the above-mentioned sources have correctly condensed the subject matter of the passage to be translated and that one of their headings can be rendered. Such things cannot be taken for granted, however, as the workshop experience discussed in these notes clearly shows. In any translation procedure it is always safer and wiser to finalize section headings at the conclusion of the drafting process.

There is a wide consensus among commentators as to the binary structure of Genesis 15. Skinner (1930:276-284) already distinguishes between (1) the theme of v. 1-6, namely, the promise of an heir, and (2) the subject matter of vv. 7-8, the promise of the land, confirmed by the covenant ceremony from v. 9 onwards. Speiser (1979:114) speaks of "two inter-related parts," with a new opening oracle in v. 7, and a broader perspective thereafter. Von Rad (1967:153) and Davidson (1979:42) concur. The tendency among Old Testament scholars today is to link v.1-6 with the Abraham patriarchal tradition (the promised descendants, a theme introduced in Genesis 12.1-5), and to place v. 7-21 within the Jacob narrative cycle (the promised land, as in Genesis 13.14-18).

Inconsistency in the narrative concerning the circumstances of its time and place can easily be detected, thus illustrating the composite nature of the passage. From a night vision under the stars, whether inside or outside a nomad's tent (v. 5), the scene moves to an area large enough for an impressive covenant ritual at sunset, with a "thick and dreadful darkness" coming over Abraham (NIV, v. 12), and the sun finally setting, and bringing darkness again (v. 17). The trusting Abram of v. 6 begins to doubt again at v. 8 and asks for another sign, as if his complaint in vv. 2-3 had not been fully and finally answered by the sign of the countless stars (v. 5).

More significant still for translation is the shift in meaning of the verbal root *yrs* from vv. 1-6 (A) to vv. 7-21 (B), in the following nuclear phrases (near-kernel rendering):

A   v.3   a servant will *inherit* from me
    v.4   not this one will *inherit* from you
          your own son will *inherit* from you
B   v.7   to give you this land to *possess* (it)
    v.8   that I shall *possess* it

The root *yrs* 'to possess' or 'to inherit' denotes two related meanings within the semantic domain of *transfer and ownership*. The one involves ownership of some object with the right of control over the use of such an object within the socially recognized customs ("possess"). The other pertains to the process of gaining possession by means of a transfer from someone who has died, generally a close relative, friend or master ("inherit"). In vv. 3-4 the process of becoming an owner is in focus, while in vv. 7-8 the resultant state of the process is highlighted.

Genesis 15.1-21 clearly deals with two literary themes, because its text rests on two distinct layers of patriarchal traditions. Yet the combination of these two traditions into a single narrative at the final stage of the text (the one which is to be translated) is no less obvious and important than its composite formation. Translators should have a clear idea of the intended unity of the story at this final editorial stage, as well as of its fragmented origins. Both stages in the transmission of the narrative are reflected in the final draft of modern versions by alternating consistency and differentiation. The same Hebrew verb used with two different meanings in the same chapter will obviously have to be rendered by two different receptor-language (RL) units. Whereas two different Hebrew phrases used with only one meaning in the same chapter should be translated by one RL phrase, e.g., *'eth ha'ares hazz 'oth lerisetah* 'this land to *possess* (it),' Genesis 15.7, and *be'eres lo' lahem* 'a land they did not *possess*,' Genesis 15.13.

Apart from the divergent use of the root *yrs*, two other Hebrew key terms occur with a similar coherent meaning in the A and B sections of Genesis 15 :

Root *ntn* 'to give' (4x)

A   v.2   what can you *give* me
    v.3   you have not *given* me (a son)
B   v.7   to *give* you (this land)

v.18   I *give* (this land)
Noun *zera'* 'descendant, descendants, posterity' (4x)

A   v.3   no *descendant*
    v.5   your *descendants*
B   v.13   your *descendants*
    v.18   to your *descendants*

The different renderings "descendant" in v. 3 and "descendants" in vv. 5, 13 and 18 (collective sense of the singular *zera'*) do not indicate two distinct meanings of the Hebrew noun, but two different usages of the same lexical unit.

Even more striking is the parallelism built into the final form of the narrative of Genesis 15 by its authors, in the shape of a double dialogue between the LORD and the patriarch.

Participants : *Yahweh* and Abram

A. *Dialogue*
    v.1   a   *I am your shield*
    v.2   b   what can you give me?
    v.3   c   a servant . . . will inherit from me
    v.5   d   *look at the heavens*

    Comment
    v.6   e   *he credited it* to him as righteousness

B   *Dialogue*
    v.7   a'   *I am the LORD*
    v.8   b'   how can I know
    v.8   c'   that I shall possess it?
    v.9   d'   *bring me a heifer*

    Comment
    v.18   e'   *the LORD made a covenant* with Abram

This brings our discussion on headings and themes back to its initial concern: How can a title be made to match the content of a pericope and to summarize its message? At the workshop plenary sessions translation teams were advised to look for a double-barrel heading, so as to avoid using subheadings in v. 1 and v. 7, possibly along the following lines:

ATD (von Rad)	*Gottes Verheissung* und *Bund mit Abraham*
ZBK (Zimmerli)	*Verheissung des Erbes* und *des Erblandes*
AncB (Speiser)	*Promise* and *Covenant*
TOB	*Promesse* et *Alliance*

None of the teams seems to have freed itself from the NIV, GNB, and RSV models, and hence to express the idea of "Promised son—promised land" in a single heading. Some of the teams have nevertheless turned the noun phrase "God's covenant" into a complete sentence, "God makes a covenant with Abram" (Chewa, Swati, Xhosa). The Tonga draft interestingly suggests "How God made a covenant with Abram."

A complete description of the content of Genesis 15 would, of course, require more than two sub-headings, for instance:

v.1-6	The Promised Descendant
v.7-9	The Promised Land (+ v.18)
v.10-11	The Covenant Ceremony Prepared
v.12-16	(Parenthesis) Delayed Fulfillment
v.17-18	The Covenant Ceremony Concluded
v.19-21	The Inhabitants of the Promised Land

2.4 Textual variants in translation

The kind of problems which textual variants present to translators has already been mentioned. Genesis 15.1-2 offers two typical examples:

2.4.1 harebeh / 'arebeh

According to BHS *harebeh* in v. 1, 'is-to-be-increaed, made-great, made-many,'[2] should be read *'arebeh* 'I-will-increase, make-great, make-many.'[3] The HOTTP report does not offer any guidance in this case, but GNB, NEB, NIV, BFC, and

---

[2] hiph. inf. of *rbh*, a rare usage, as qualificative of *sekareka*, "your reward, your blessing." See Westermann in BKAT.

[3] hiph. impf, 1 p.s., with the Samaritan Pentateuch.

BHD have opted for the rendering "I-will-increase," with NEB and NIV indicating the equivalent of "is-to-be-increased," in a footnote.

The choice between the reading *harebeh* and the variant *'arebeh* is but a preliminary step for translators. Should they wish to keep the infinitive of the MT (the more difficult reading), they would still have to transform the phrase *sekareka harebeh* at the kernel level and try successively, "Your reward/blessing will be very great, You will be greatly rewarded/blessed, Yahweh will greatly reward/bless you, (and in direct speech) I will greatly reward/bless you." In other words, the best way to render the *meaning* of the MT (hiph. inf.) in the context of Genesis 15.1 is by using the 1st pers. sing. "I-will-greatly-reward/bless you," as if one were rendering the Samaritan Pentateuch variant (hiph. impf.).[4] The footnotes in NIV en NEB amount to an apology for rendering the Sam. Pent. variant in the text and are not really necessary.

Nearly half of the translation teams did not hesitate to render the phrase *sekareka harebeh* in the 1st pers. sing. (Chewa, Nama, S. Ndebele, S. Sotho, Swati, Tonga, Xhosa, Zulu), as "I shall greatly reward/bless you." Others have reconstructed the expression as "Your reward/blessing will be very great," or "You will have many blessings" (Herero, Tsonga, Venda). For translating *sakar* as "blessing" rather than "reward," see 3.3 below.

2.4.2 ubhen meseq bethi

This difficult phrase in v. 2 confronted the translation teams with another challenge, this time with clear sociolinguistic implications. As the footnotes of NIV and GNB show, the expression (a *hapax legomenon*) is puzzling and has often been declared "inexplicable" by commentators. Such discouraging textual assessments are of little assistance to translators, who unlike commentators cannot replace an obscure Hebrew phrase by three convenient little dots.

All the ancient versions show diversities at this point. Some take *ubhen* in the literal sense of "sons of" (LXX *huios*; V *filius*), and *meseq* as the proper name of a person (LXX "Masek my female slave"). It could also be a geographical name, and the phrase could refer to someone from a place called *Meseq*. In popular traditions, secondary characters in a narrative tend to be given proper names. Compare the "wise men from the East" in Mt. 2.1, later becoming the legendary three kings, Gaspar, Melchior and Balthasar. "Eliezer the

---

[4] One could also take the phrase as a second predicate to *'anoki*, like V: *ego merces tua magna nimis*.

Damascene" of v. 3 would be another identification of Abram's domestic servant, named in a marginal gloss, which would have been later incorporated into the text. Others consider *meseq* as a modification of *mesek* possession, inheritance and take *ubhen* in the distinct meaning of "member of a group or class," hence *ubhen meseq* 'possessor, inheritor, heir,' as in v. 3, where *bhen bethi* refers to "a member of my household, a domestic servant." This last interpretation has been adopted overwhelmingly by the Western versions. Yet TOB (p. 66), following Aquila, has noted that *meseq* could derive from the root *sqh* 'to pour a liquid, a libation,' and be related to the noun *masqeh* 'butler, cup-bearer.' In the Ancient Near East an heir through biological descent or through adoption not only takes over the material property of the deceased but also looks after it. Even if adopted, he is also the person responsible for "providing a proper burial for his parents" by offering libations at the grave (Von Rad 1952:158; Davidson 1979:43). The curse of childlessness, in Israel as well as in traditional Africa, is therefore linked with the absence of future officiants at the family burial grounds.

A number of workshop drafts render the phrase *ubhen meseq* with a comparable idiom, namely "the one who will *eat* Abram's property" after his death. S. Sotho uses a nominalized verb *mojalefa ea ka*; others have a full phrase, as in Tsonga, *la nga ta dya ndzhaka ya mina*; S. Ndebele, *ozakudla lilifa lami*; Venda, *a no do la ifa langa*; and Xhosa, *yindlalifa lam*. The rhetorical similarity could not be clearer, as an expression of functional correspondence. The eldest son as heir (or the son of the deceased's sister in Chewa matrilineal society; see further at paragraph 4.2) plays a prominent role in all southern-African societies, at a funeral and its manifold rituals. This is why the so-called "inexplicable" *ubhen meseq* can receive at least one tentative explanation in an Ancient Near Eastern or an African context. The phrase must in any case be translated.

As for the gloss *hu dammeseq 'eliezer*, unfairly described as "stupid" by Skinner (1930:279), one feels that it would not have allegedly passed from the margin into the text of Genesis 15.2, if it had not previously (at a preliterate stage) belonged to an oral tradition, easily remembered because of the striking alliteration *meseq-dammeseq*. Whatever the transmission or editorial truth might be in this case, the fact is that the phrase "Eliezer from Damascus" has found its natural rendering in all the workshop drafts, and this, despite its doubtful Hebrew base (lit. "the Damascus Eliezer," not "the Damascene Eliezer," or "Eliezer from Damascus").

2.5 Semantic relations

The following step in the workshop approach to the text of Genesis 15 consisted in a simple analysis of its narrative coherence. During the preparation period the participants were introduced to a literal English rendering of the Hebrew source, with nuclear sentences isolated and suitably indented to show their relations of coordination or subordination. A preliminary grasp of the semantic *relations* linking the meaningful units of the text was deemed essential for the reconstruction process to be undertaken later in the day by the various teams.

In the simplified layout (so-called "exploded text") reproduced below, each syntactic cluster, or *colon*, starts at the margin with a basic segment, or *matrix*. The *extended features* of that basic unit are then spread on first, second, third, or more indentations.

The word order of the Hebrew text and the sequence of its meaningful units have been maintained, since the aim is to illustrate the obvious need to transform the surface structure of the source text in translation. In general, a *hyphenated segment* corresponds to one Hebrew lexical unit. The only exceptions to the reproduction of the Hebrew word sequence in the following layout concern *demonstratives* (e.g., v. 1 "After these things," for Hebrew "After things these"), or the sequence verb-noun in *verbal sentences* (e.g., v. 2 "and Abram said," for Hebrew "and-he-said Abram").

A few *bracketed* words and phrases have been added to the text, to indicate the kind of semantic relations which can be discerned between the constituent units. These relations are further described in the right-hand margin. A bracketed indicator may sometimes express the denotative meaning of a Hebrew *waw* (e.g., v. 2 *we'anoki* 'since I-myself').

GENESIS 15.1-6 THE PROMISED DESCENDANTS

v.1, 1.1	after these things	circumstance
.2	there-was a-word-of Yahweh to Abram	matrix
.3	in-a-vision	manner
.4	saying	anaphoric
.5	do-not fear, Abram	content 5-7
.6	(because) I (am) a-shield to-you	reason
.7	(and so) your-reward (is)	
	to-be-increased greatly	result

v.2, 2.1 and Abram said	matrix (unfold.)
.2 my-Lord GOD	phatic
.3 what (could) you-give me	content 3-5
.4 (since) I-myself am-going childless	cause
.5 and (so) the heir of my-house	
(is) he (from) Damascus Eliezer	result
v.3, 3.1 and Abram said	matrix (unfold.)
.2 look to-me you have not given	
a-descendant	content 2-3
.3 and (thus) -see a-son-of my-house	
is-inheriting (from) me	result
v.4, 4.1 and-see a-word-of Yahweh to-him	matrix (unfold.)
.2 saying	anaphoric
.3 not this-one will-inherit-(from)-you	content 3-5
.4 but only he-who comes-out	contrast +
of-your-bowels	character 4-5
.5 he will-inherit-(from)-you	
v.5, 5.1 and-he-took him outside	circumstance
.2 and-he-said	matrix (unfold.)
.3 look please towards-heaven	content 3-5
.4 and-count (then) the-stars	purpose
.5 if you-are-able to-count	
them	condition
6.1 and-he-said to-him	matrix (unfold.)
.2 such will-be your-descendants	content
v.6, 7.1 and-he-trusted in-Yahweh	matrix (unfold.)
.2 and-(so)-he-credited-it to-him	result
.3 (as) righteousness	character

During the preparation period the translation teams were encouraged to reconstruct the narrative of Genesis 15 on the basis of the kernel layout, and especially (a) to express the implicit relations linking the Hebrew nuclear segments and (b) if necessary, to re-arrange these segments in order to produce a coherent story in the RL. These objectives seem to have been well understood, as shown by the following three examples.

2.5.1 *mah titten li* 'what (could) you-give me'

Various reconstruction possibilities arise from the above ambiguous phrase in v. 2 (segment 2.3). This can be understood as a genuine question, and *mah* can be taken as an interrogative pronoun. Yet such a straightforward query is unlikely in the context of the dialogue between Yahweh and Abram. RSV "What wilt thou give me?" and TOB *Que me donneras-tu* miss the point. The question should be understood as rhetorical with a potential connotation, and *mah* should be taken as an adverb: "What (on earth) could you give me!" or "What is the use of you giving me something!"

This restrictive, potential meaning is variously expressed in the model versions, namely by NIV "*What can* you give me?"; GNB "*What good* will your reward do to me?"; BFC *A quoi bon me donner quelque chose?*; BHD *Womit willst du mich denn belohnen?* In the workshop drafts, a similar associative meaning of doubt or objection is expressed through various stylistic means. Chewa says "What kind of blessing will you give me?" Herero changes the rhetorical question into a statement, "Your reward will be of no use to me!" Others, like Nama, S. Ndebele, S. Sotho, N. Sotho, Tswana, and Venda, translate by "What can (could) you give me?" Xhosa and Swati render this question as "How will that help me?" Tsonga makes use of the potential mood *Xana u to ndzi nyika yini . . . hikuva a ndzo va na n'wana* 'What could you possibly give me . . . since I simply do not have a child!' The indicative mood would be *Xana u ta ndzi nyika yini . . . hikuva a ndzi na n'wana.*

With this potential or restrictive connotation implicit in the Hebrew *mah*, but expressed in translation, a logical sequence has been established between the incredible promise of the LORD in v. 1 and the painful objection of Abram, who so far remains childless.

2.5.2 *we'anoki holek* '(since) I-myself am-going'

The next problem of semantic relations concerns the translation of the initial *waw*. In the above phrase (segment 2.4), Abram now indicates the reasons for the doubts expressed in segment 2.3, and some of the model versions have therefore rendered the phrase as a causal subordinate, as in GNB "*since* I have no children"; NIV "*since* I remain childless"; von Rad *da ich doch kinderlos wandere*.

Other versions have chosen to ignore the *waw*, and thus skipped the causal relation, as in NAV *Ek sal kinderloos sterf*, NEB "I have no standing among men," BFC *Je suis sans enfant*.

Chewa translates this relation with a rhetorical question, "Am I not without a child up to now?" Herero, Kung, Mbukushu, Swati, Tonga, Tsonga, and Venda express the subordination with a conjunction. S. Ndebele uses the subordinate negative mood *njingamntwa nje* 'I not having a child,' and Xhosa renders the phrase with the same stylistic device *ndingenabantwana nje*? 'I not having children' 'while I do not have children.' Finally, Kwanyama and Nama prefer to start the kernel sentence 2.4 as a new statement, as NAV and other models have done.

For the translation of the initial *waw* in Abram's reply (seg. 2.4), there are thus no less than four different syntactical possibilities, most probably all available in the languages represented at the workshop. In the oral approach of a translation team these four possible renderings of the Hebrew base will have been tested as alternatives, and one of them selected as the best for the specific literary context. The great disadvantage of the lonely paper-bound translator is the inevitable reduction in the range of stylistic alternatives coming to his or her mind during the drafting process. As the Tsonga proverb says, "One single finger cannot lift a grain of maize!" or "The hand cannot wash itself!"

2.5.3 *wayyahesebeha* 'and-(so)-he-credited-it'

There is another example in v. 6 (segment 7.2) of a semantic relationship which is implied in Hebrew and which should be made explicit, namely, the logical link between Abram's trust and Yahweh's gracious response, all "hidden" in the prefix *waw* and the suffix *ha* of *wayyahesebeha*.

GNB correctly renders "and because of this, the LORD was pleased," in contrast with the ambiguous translation of NIV "and he (who?) credited it to him (who?)."

The workshop drafts of Herero, Mbukushu, Swati, Tsonga, Venda, and Xhosa have all translated with expressions which show a sub-ordination of consequence or result in segment 7.2, namely, "Therefore/and for this/and as a consequence/that is why . . . the LORD regarded/accepted/considered Abram as . . ."

2.6 Organization of dialogue

2.6.1 Direct speech markers

For the dialogue between Yahweh and Abram, the use of the direct speech seems to come naturally. A phrase similar to the Hebrew anaphoric formula *lemor* (v. 1, v. 4 segments 1.4 and 4.2) is shared by a number of the languages from the subcontinent represented at the workshop. It is a common stylistic feature, almost unknown to Western languages. Whereas the formula sounds pleonastic in English, it comes naturally and in fact appears stylistically indispensable, at least in the following four languages, as a marker of direct speech:

Chewa, *Abramu adayankhako . . . kuti*: 'A. answered saying/he said'
Mbukushu, *Ko kwipura Abrahama . . . eshi*:   "   "   "   "
Tsonga, *Abrama a hlamula . . . a ku*:   "   "   "   "
Xhosa, *Uphendula wathi uAbram*: "He answered he said Abram"

2.6.2 Identifying the participants

The two main participants are identified, either by the oracle formula *haya debhar YHWH 'el* or by the standard reply formula *wayyomer 'abhram*. In segments 5.1, 6.1, 7.1 and 7.2, however, the participants are implied in Hebrew and should preferably be identified to avoid ambiguity, particularly with the change of subject between 7.1 and 7.2 "and-he-trusted (Abram) . . . and-(so)-he-credited (Yahweh)." GNB, NEB, NAV, BFC have chosen to be explicit, in contrast with RSV and NIV, which remain ambiguous. BHD has completely reconstructed the verse and made Abram its only grammatical subject.

The workshop teams have followed the explicit models and identified Abram as the subject of *wehe'emin*, at the beginning of segment 7.1 (v. 6).

Another participant, namely, the silent Eliezer, may also need to be identified in segment 4.3, *lo' yiraseka zeh*, as in GNB, "This *slave Eliezer* will not inherit your property." This has served as a model for Herero, S. Ndebele, Tsonga, Venda, and Xhosa, which all mention Eliezer.

As for the fourth participant in the narrative, namely, the anonymous commentator in v. 6 and v. 18, there is no need and in fact no possibility to identify him in this particular context.

3. Words in context

A number of lexical units were pinpointed during the preparatory session and discussed at length in the groups. In all cases, what became obvious was the need to understand and render each lexical unit, not in isolation, but within its immediate context and in a way consistent with the general flow of the narrative.

3.1 "In-a-vision"

The word *mahazeh* in segment 1.3 can be understood as an objective revelation coming from Yahweh, or subjectively, as something seen by Abram in a personal experience. Translators must make a decision. GNB chooses the second meaning by translating, "Abram had a vision." The Xhosa draft follows GNB. The subjective usage of *mahazeh* may be found in Ezekiel 13.7 in a reference to false prophetic dreams; but apart from Genesis 15.1 the other two occurrences of the word, namely, Numbers 24.4 and 16, refer to an objective divine communication. Likewise, the root *hzh* belongs to prophetic language and is often found in oracles of salvation with a typical sequence of interpellation, promise, and confirmation. Here, Yahweh takes the initiative, calls his servant Abram, promises him an heir, confirms the promise with an injunction to look at the stars, and expects the patriarch's trustful response. All this points to an objective meaning of the phrase *bamahazeh* in the context of Genesis 15.1-6.

Moreover, the "vision" in Genesis 15.1 is linked with the transmission of a divine message, with a *debhar YHWH*. The LORD appears to Abram and speaks with him; he shows himself by addressing him. The majority of the workshop teams chose to translate "vision" in this objective way. They therefore rendered the phrase "there-was a-word-of YHWH in-a-vision" in a manner appropriate to a context of sovereign divine initiative addressed to Abram. The following pattern has been generally followed, "Yahweh showed himself to/ appeared to . . . Abram (in a vision) and said to him/ by speaking to him" (Chewa, Nama Tsonga, Kwanyama). The Herero draft says, "The LORD spoke to Abram, thus revealing himself." Kung, S. Sotho, N. Sotho, and Tswana render, "The LORD spoke to Abram by means of a dream" (he does not see God, he hears him). Once again, the diversity of possible stylistic formulas is remarkable, as soon as the strict adherence to the Hebrew word sequence is abandoned and a proper reconstruction takes place.

3.2 "I (am) a-shield to-you"

The Western model versions tend to drop the metaphor of the shield, probably because of its medieval, obsolete connotation. They render the meaning of "protection," either by a noun: BFC, *Je suis ton protecteur* or by a verb: BHD, *Ich werde dich beschützen*, NAV *Ek beskerm jou*, GNB *I will shield you from danger*.

In a southern-African context the oxhide shields of warfare are part of a recent military tradition. The metaphor has therefore generally been kept (Herero, Kwanyama, Mbukushu, Swati, Tsonga, Venda). Sometimes a qualifier has been added, "a shield to protect you" (Chewa, S. Ndebele, S. Sotho, Zulu). The Nama and Xhosa drafts prefer to follow GNB and say "I will protect you," with the remark that the "young people feel the 'shield' to be an unknown word."

One finds here a clear illustration of the importance of the cultural setting in translation.

3.3 "Your-reward"

The idea of a "reward" or "recompense" or even "payment" seems out of place in the immediate context of Yahweh's dialogue with Abram. It is true that most of the occurrences of the Hebrew word *sakar* belong to the semantic field of "commercial transaction." Like the image of the "shield," it could also be used in a military context as a soldier's hire.

Nevertheless, in the narrative of Genesis 15, what could constitute Abram's right to such a "wage" or "reward"? Von Rad (1952:154) speaks here of a "free gift of God," as in Isaiah 40.10; 62.11; and Jeremiah 31.16. This points to another, distinct meaning of *sakar*, namely, a "gracious gift," a "divine blessing." Most of the workshop drafts have chosen to express this meaning by "blessing" (Chewa, Herero, Kwanyama, Tsonga, Swati). Others render the same idea by means of a verbal phrase, "I will greatly bless you."

3.4 'mn, hsb, sedaqa

The translation of these three key-terms of v. 6 should be compared in the model versions and in the workshop exercises, but such an analysis dealing with one of the central verses in the Bible could form a chapter of its own. The following summary will have to suffice. Most of the workshop drafts have rendered the three terms in a similar way. Abram *trusts* in Yahweh, who *accepts* the patriarch (as a sacrificial animal is "accepted" by the temple priest) as his *rightful partner*.

The root -*lung*- is shared by a number of southern African languages. It often carries the meaning of "correct behavior" or of "legal correctness." In this particular narrative, however, as a concluding comment to the dialogue between Yahweh and his servant, the root -*lung*- describes a *normal relationship* between the Sovereign LORD and a responsive Abram, as unequal but mutually-trusting partners. It is found in the drafts of Mbukushu, S. Ndbele, Swati, Tsonga, and Xhosa.

Once again, the crucial factor for translators is not the isolated lexical unit and its so-called "basic" dictionary meaning. What really matters are various usages of one of its meanings. Alternately, one is dealing with distinct meanings of that unit in different contexts, whether internal (narrative, themes) or external (life-setting, cultural milieu).

4. Rhetorical features

Some of the stylistic devices found in Genesis 15.1-6 and their translation have already been discussed, e.g., the shared anaphoric formula "he answered . . . he said"; the need to identify the participants in a dialogue; and the various natural ways for translating the Hebrew particle *waw*.

Two more idiomatic expressions with cultural connotations should finally be noted in the present analysis.

4.1 "I-myself am-going childless"

Should one take the Hebrew participle *holek* as a metonymy or as a euphemism for "to die"? Abram would say: "I am going childless to the grave." Or should the expression be understood as referring to a continuous state, "I continue being childless / I remain childless"?

The versions are divided. NAV and Skinner, with LXX, translate "to die," while NIV, NEB, GNB and BFC, with V (*vadam*), as well as nearly all the workshop drafts, render "to remain childless / childless until now."

With the idea of "curse" or "great misfortune" attached to childlessness, and the meaning of "dying" for the root *hlk* in Psalm 39.13, one would tend to translate *holek* here as "I am going to the grave," keeping in mind the primary duty of an heir to see to the proper burial of his parents (sociocultural factor) in the Ancient Near East and in Israel.

4.2 "He-who comes-out of-your-bowels"

Most of the translation teams, guided by GNB, BHD and NAV, have correctly refrained from a literal translation of the Hebrew idiomatic expression. They say, "your true child / your own son / your real offspring / a child born of you" (Chewa, Herero, Nama, S. Ndebele, Tsonga, Venda). Xhosa suggests an ideophone, "your son, exactly, *ngqo!*" Others would like to translate with an idiom of their own, related to Hebrew but not identical (or is it a biblical idiom which has somehow penetrated into the languages concerned and undergone a slight semantic shift there?). Swati translates by *indvodzana yakho lephuma elukhalweni lwakho* 'the son of yours who comes from the waist of yours.' S. Sotho similarly says *more ya tswang thekeng la hao* 'a son coming from your loins.'

Any translators aware of the need for contextual perspectives will consider not only the mode of inheritance in Israel and among her neighbors, but, for their target constituencies, they will also pay attention to the cultural implication of the theme of Genesis 15.1-6, the promised heir. Can an estate be "eaten" by the eldest son of the deceased (S. and N. Sotho, for instance)? Or should it be divided among all the children, the youngest one inheriting the house (Tswana)? In the case of a matrilineal and matrilocal kinship system, should the inheritance go to the eldest son of the deceased's sister (Chewa)? Any radical departure in the receptor culture from the Israelite rule of primogenital inheritance should be indicated in a footnote or spelled out in a glossary entry.

5. Conclusions

The main conclusions to be drawn from the translation workshop exercise on Genesis 15 as described above have already been noted at the beginning of this chapter. They are basically of four kinds:

5.1 The appropriateness of *oral procedures* in any translation team method, where "translating aloud" forms part of the basic approach to the text.

5.2 The necessity to evaluate *textual variants* in the source text (BHS apparatus, HOTTP Preliminary and Interim Report, and other textual guides) from the point of view of a project's translation principles. A translation team should have the courage to make the inevitable exegetical and theological choices at every step, with a due sense of responsibility toward what is most likely to be an ecumenical receptor community.

5.3 The usefulness of *comparing* lexical units, syntactic resources, and rhetorical features in a workshop experience where translators in cognate languages with a similar sociocultural background, work together on the same biblical source material.

5.4 The need to avoid not only a literal and therefore meaningless rendering of Hebrew lexical and syntactical units but also a mere imitation of Western versions in the reconstruction process. Models should not become the base (translating GNB instead of BHS!), nor should a literal rendering of the MT in any of the model versions prevent translators from working with imagination, creativity, and above all sensitivity to their own sociolinguistic environment.

Hebrew Text

       BHS   Biblia Hebraica Stuttgartensia

Quoted versions

LXX	Septuagint
V	Vulgate
RSV	Revised Standard Version
NIV	New International Version
GNB	Good News Bible
NEB	New English Bible
NAV	Die Bybel Nuwe Vertaling (Afrikaans New Bible Translation)
TOB	Traduction Oecumnique de la Bible (French Ecumenical Bible Translation)
BFC	La Bible en Français Courant (The Bible in Presentday French)
BHD	Die Bibel in Heutigem Deutsch (Today's German Bible)

Collected drafts

(Languages from the African Sub-Continent represented at Translation Workshop)

Chewa (Chichewa)	Swati (Siswati)
Herero (Otjiherero)	Southern Sotho
Kung (Gobabis)	Northern Sotho

Kwanyama	Tswana
Kwangali	Tonga
Mbukushu	Tsonga
Nama	Venda
Southern Ndebele	Xhosa
	Zulu

Commentaries referred to

ICC   Skinner, J. 1930. "Genesis," 2nd ed., in the *International Critical Commentary*, Edinburgh: Clark.

ATD   von Rad, G. 1967. "Das Erste Buch Mose," in *Das Alte Testament Deutsch*, Gottingen: Vandenhoeck und Ruprecht.

ZBK   Zimmerli, W. 1. 1976. "Mose 12-25, Abraham," in *Zürcher Bibelkommentare*, Zürich: Theologischer Verlag.

CBC   Davidson, R. 1979. "Genesis 12-50," in the *Cambridge Bible Commentary*, London: Cambridge University Press.

AncB   Speiser, E.A. 1979. "Genesis, " in *The Anchor Bible*, New York: Doubleday.

BKAT   Westermann, G. 1981. "Genesis," in *Biblischer Kommentar Altes Testament*, Band I/2, Neukirchen-Vluyn: Neukirchener Verlag.

<u>Samples of workshop drafts</u>[5]
Genesis 15.1-6

<u>Chewa</u> (Chichewa)

v.1 *Pambuyo pake Chàuta adaonekera Abramu namuza kuti,*
     Afterwards Yahweh appeared to Abram and said to him

   "Iwe Abramu, usachite mantha, chifukwa Ine ndine chishango
   "You Abram, do not be afraid, because I am a shield

   chokuteteza, ndiponso ndidzakupatsa madalitso aakulu."
   protecting you, and I shall give you blessings great."

v.2 *Koma Abramu adayankhako pakunena kuti,*
     But Abram answered something by saying that,

   "Ha, Inu Ambuye Chauta mudzandipatsa madalitso otani?
   "Come on, you Lord GOD you will give me blessings of what kind?

   Suja mpaka pano mwana ndilibe kodi? Ndipo wodzalandira
   Isn't it up to now a child I am without? And the one to receive

   cholowa changa kodi si Eliezere wa ku Damasikoyu?
   inheritance of me isn't it Eliezer from Damascus this?

<u>Herero</u> (Otjiherero)

v.3 *Ove ko ndzi pere orukwato (ovanatje); ngu ma rire*
     You have given me no offspring; the one to

---

[5] The interlinear English back-translations are the ones suggested by the secretaries of the various translation teams during the afternoon drafting sessions. They obviously operate at different levels of literalness, and they have not been checked or edited. Nor has any attempt been made to harmonize them.

omurumate weta randje iumwe wovakarere vandje."
inherit my property will be one of my servants."

v.4 *Muhona arire tje mu riri a tja : "Ingwi Elieser kangu ma*
Then the LORD answered him: "It is not this Eliezer

rire omurumate weta roye; omuatje woye omuini ngu mo
who is to be your heir; your son whom you will bring

kwata ongu ma rumata ouini woye."
forth he will inherit your property."

Nama

v.5 *Ob ge !khŭba !augab ǁga =|toa-ŭ bi tsî ge mî:*
(Then) the LORD took him outside and said :

"|Homma !oa kôkhâi, îts |gamirode !goa,
"Look up towards the sky, so that (and) count the stars,

!goa di ǁkhats koa. ǁNas kôseb ge sa suriba mî =|gui."
if you can count them. So many (As many as that) will your offspring be."

v.6 *Ob ge Abramma !khŭba ge =|gom, tsî !khub ge ǁîb |kha =|khî =|âixa.*
(Then) Abram believed the LORD, and the LORD was pleased with him.

or: *tsî !khŭb ge ǁîsa =|hanuaisib ase ge !goa ba bi.*
and the LORD counted it as righteousness to him

Swati (Siswati)

v.1 *Emvakwaloko livi laSimakadze lefika ku-Abrama ngembono*
After that the voice of the LORD came to Abram through a vision

latsi
and it said

"Abrama, ungesabi, ngisihlangu sakho,
"Abram, do not be afraid, I am shield yours,

esibusiso sakho lesikhulu."
and the blessing of yours which is great."

v.2 *Kodvwa Abrama watsi : "Awu, Simakadze Nkulunkulu,*
But Abram said : "O, Lord God,

kutangisita ngani loko, ngobe seloku anginamntfwana.
it will help me how that, because till now I have no child.

Indlalifa yami kutakuba ngu-Eliyezeri waseDamaseko."
The heir of mine it will be this Eliezer of Damascus."

Tsonga

v.3 *Abrama a tlhela a ku: "A wu ndzi nyikanga n'wana,*
Abram continued and said: "You have not given me a child,

kutani hlonga leri nga laha mutini wa mina,
therefore a slave who is here in my village,

hi rona ri nga ta va mudyandzhaka.
"it is he who will be heir ('inheritance-eater')."

v.4 *Kutani HOSI Xikwembu xi ku ka Abrama: "Munhu loyi*
Then the LORD said to Abram: "This man

Eliezere, a hi yena a nga ta va mudyandzhaka ya wena,
Eliezer, it is not he who will be your heir ('inheritance-eater'),

kambe n'wana wa wena wa xiviri, hi yena a nga ta dya
but your son, your own, it is he who will eat

ndzhaka ya wena."
your inheritance."

Venda

v.5 *Muṋe washu a dzhia Aburamu, a bvela nae nnḓa a ri,*
The LORD took Abram, he went out with him and said,

"Sedza ṱadulu u vhale naledzi. U nga dzi vhala dzoṱhe
"Look up and count the stars. Can you count them

naa?" Ndi hone a tshi mu vhudza a ri, "Vhaduhulu vhau na
all?" And he told him he said, "Your grand-child-

vhone vha do vha vha si na mbalo."
ren they also they will be without number."

v.6 *Aburamu a fulufhela Muṋe washu, ndi zwe Muṋe washu*
Abram put his trust in the LORD, that is why the LORD

a mu vhona e muvhuya.
saw him as righteous.

Chapter 4

Translating a New Testament Narrative Text: Luke 1.1-25

Johannes P. Louw

As proposed in chapter 1, a translator should never aim at rendering the Bible (or for that matter, any other source text) in such a way that the hearer or reader merely understands the translated text. No, the aim should be that the reader will not misunderstand the message of the source text. Apart from cryptic texts, people generally understand, or at least think they understand, what they read or hear, but their understanding is not necessarily in line with what the author of the text presumably wanted to communicate. This applies equally to the source text of the first author as well as to the translation produced by the translator, who is, in a sense, the author of the translation. The translator should, therefore, be extremely careful not to misunderstand the source text and then, again, be extremely careful in presenting a translation that will not be misunderstood by the hearer or reader.

A text is not a mere string of words lined up in sequence. It is a structured organization formulated in accordance with the syntactic and rhetorical conventions of a particular language by utilizing the semantic components of the syntactic and lexical units and selecting, on the basis of style, specific configurations—all of which are structured in a discourse framework. The multiplicity of features and their multidimensional relations are probably the prime reason for the original text being open to misunderstanding. The translator, therefore, should not attempt to render a source-language text into a receptor language unless every effort has been made to avoid misunderstanding it. Helps for translators such as translators' handbooks, grammars, dictionaries, commentaries, etc. generally devote a good deal of attention to syntax and semantics, and, quite correctly, they do so within the framework of the historical and cultural setting of the text. Rhetorical considerations of style have received some attention, but very little has been done to grasp the structural organization of the discourse despite the fact that discourse analysis is no longer a newcomer.

Though it is true that translators' guides at times pay some attention to the discourse structure of the source text, little is said about the paragraphing of the source text, which generally follows either an age-old tradition that was based on a somewhat superficial content analysis, or is a rather haphazard series of paragraphs. In such cases traditional sections are often subdivided into a number of rather small subparagraphs, while the overall pattern of the larger sections is generally neglected. There are, however, in most instances a number of smaller internal breaks which differ considerably from one translation to another. Bible translations rarely show traces of serious and detailed consideration being given to the structure of the translated text. Our convention of dividing the Bible text into a series of chapters and verses has no doubt much to do with creating an unnatural segmentation of the text. Unfortunately many translators do not realize the extent to which readers are conditioned in their understanding of the translated text by the layout of the text, especially in terms of its paragraphing.

Paragraphing is, of course, not all that is at stake; it is merely one of the issues that calls for attention when the discourse structure of a text is seriously considered. Another very important factor is focus, which involves foregrounding and backgrounding. Here, various rhetorical devices, such as repetitions, omissions, and shifts in expectancies, play an important role. These feature in any discourse function as important prompters to condition the understanding of the reader or hearer.

Understanding is basically a matter of recognizing relations based on patterns of similarity and contrast. Therefore, it is essentially a procedure of comparison. If well done, one can arrive at what may be called a primary reading of a text, which takes into account all the linguistic and paralinguistic features, as well as the extralinguistic features related to the historical and cultural setting of a text. In order not to misunderstand the message, the reader or hearer must be guided by the form and format of the text in such a way as to recognize overtly or covertly the fundamental semantic elements of the message.

Accordingly, no translator should ever undertake any translation of a text unless he or she is thoroughly acquainted with the structure of the entire passage. This involves not only the text as a whole but also the different units within the text. Because of the difficulty of grasping the message of a complete text without taking into consideration its constituent parts—and conversely one cannot fully appreciate the role of the parts without a grasp of the whole—it is necessary to alternate continually between the parts and the whole. This involves checking and rechecking one's analyses in order to understand without misunderstanding.

To illustrate the actual process required as preliminary to any meaningful translation, two sample passages, one from Luke and the other from Romans, may be usefully considered in this and the following chapter.

The first full sentence in the Greek text of the Gospel according to Luke includes verses 1-4. The first step in analysis requires a syntactic breakdown of the sentence in order to see how the constituent units are organized. Though the skilled translator may be able to do this fairly quickly, it is necessary for an analytical methodology to move slowly step by step in order to illustrate the various items that must be considered.

The Greek text with an interlinear gloss is as follows:

ἐπειδήπερ πολλοὶ ἐπεχείρησαν ἀνατάξασθαι διήγησιν περὶ
because many have undertaken to compile a narrative of

τῶν πεπληροφορημένων ἐν ἡμῖν πραγμάτων καθὼς
the which have been accomplished among us things just as

παρέδοσαν ἡμῖν οἱ ἀπ' ἀρχῆς αὐτόπται
they delivered to us those who from the beginning eyewitnesses

καὶ ὑπηρέται γενόμενοι τοῦ λόγου ἔδοξε κἀμοὶ
and ministers were of the word it seemed good to me also

παρηκολουθηκότι ἄνωθεν πᾶσιν ἀκριβῶς καθεξῆς σοι
having followed for a long time all things closely orderly for you

γράψαι κράτιστε Θεόφιλε ἵνα ἐπιγνῷς περὶ
to write most excellent Theophilus that you may know concerning

ὧν κατηχήθης λόγων τὴν ἀσφάλειαν.
of which you have been taught things the certainty.

The following analysis of the Greek text takes into account three translations which have been influential in translating the Bible in many areas in Africa south of the equator and one translation which has had considerable influence in South Africa. However, the principles and procedures involved are applicable to translating in general.

Revised Standard Version (RSV): "Inasmuch as many have undertaken to compile a narrative of the things which have been accomplished among us, just as they were delivered to us by those who from the beginning were eyewitnesses and ministers of the word, it seemed good to me also, having followed all things closely for some time past, to write an orderly account for you, most excellent Theophilus, that you may know the truth concerning the things of which you have been informed."

New International Version (NIV): "Many have undertaken to draw up an account of the things that have been fulfilled among us, just as they were handed down to us by those who from the first were eyewitnesses and servants of the word. Therefore, since I myself have carefully investigated everything from the beginning, it seemed good also to me to write an orderly account for you, most excellent Theophilus so that you may know the certainty of the things you have been taught."

Today's English Version (TEV): "Dear Theophilus: Many people have done their best to write a report of the things that have taken place among us. They wrote what we have been told by those who saw these things from the beginning and who proclaimed the message. And so, Your Excellency, because I have carefully studied all these matters from their beginning, I thought it would be good to write an orderly account for you. I do this so that you will know the full truth about everything which you have been taught."

New Afrikaans Version (NAV):

Hooggeagte Teofilus! Daar is baie wat onderneem het om 'n verhaal te
Honorable Theolphilus! Many undertook to write a report of the

skrywe van die dinge wat onder ons gebeur het. Hulle het dit opgeteken
things that happened among us. They compiled it as it was transmitted

soos dit aan ons oorgelewer is deur die mense wat van die begin af
to us by those who have been eyewitnesses from the beginning and

ooggetuies en dienaars van die Woord was. Daarom het ek dit ook
also ministers of the Word. Therefore I also thought it would be

goedgedink om self alles stap vir stap van voor af te ondersoek
good to investigate everything from the beginning and to write

en die verhaal noukeurig in die regte volgorde vir u neer te
up the report carefully in proper order for

skryf. So kan u te wete kom dat die dinge waaroor u onderrig
you. Thus you can know that what you have been taught

is, heeltemal betroubaar is.
is fully reliable.

In the first place, the Greek text is so constructed that the syntactic matrix ἔδοξε κἀμοί 'it seemed good to me also' is in the middle. The matrix is preceded by a fairly long clause introduced by ἐπειδήπερ 'because,' stating a reason which includes everything up to τοῦ λόγου 'of the word.' The matrix is then followed by two clauses. The first links grammatically to the matrix by means of a participial construction παρηκολουθηκότι 'having followed,' which enlarges syntactically upon the phrase κἀμοί 'to me also,' though semantically it describes the methodology and content of the message conveyed to the addressee. The second clause introduced by ἵνα 'that' states the purpose of the communication. It is also important to note that the clause preceding the matrix moves immediately from reason to content, namely, "a narrative of the things which have been accomplished among us," and then to methodology: καθώς 'just as.' The content is resumed in the first clause following the matrix: πᾶσιν 'all things.'

The syntactic structure of the first sentence in Luke's Gospel is semantically quite complex since it includes a number of overlapping features: reason-content-methodology-matrix-content-methodology-addressee-purpose. The content items are referentially similar, but the methodology refers to different types of agents: on the one hand, "eyewitnesses and ministers of the word" and on the other hand, the author of the Gospel. Note also that the reason for and the purpose of writing the Gospel are stated at the beginning and the end of the sentence. As such, they gain in focus along with the author, who is the agent of the matrix: "it seemed good to me" "I thought/judged/decided that it would be good to."

The above analysis may now be diagrammed as follows:

> It seemed good to me also
>
> ```
> ┌──────⟶  why = reason
> └──────⟶  why = purpose
> ```

In other words: I have decided to write to you, Theophilus; there is a reason for
                    my account, there is also a purpose to it.

In translating this first sentence in Luke, it is necessary to highlight these basic features of the message. Note that in the Greek text the author has arranged the three elements as reason + statement + purpose. This is fine Greek style but may not be acceptable in a particular target language. In terms of Greek style this arrangement foregrounds the three elements. Other stylistic devices may do the same in other languages.

The diagram may be enlarged by filling out the details of the structural units along with the semantic values of each item.

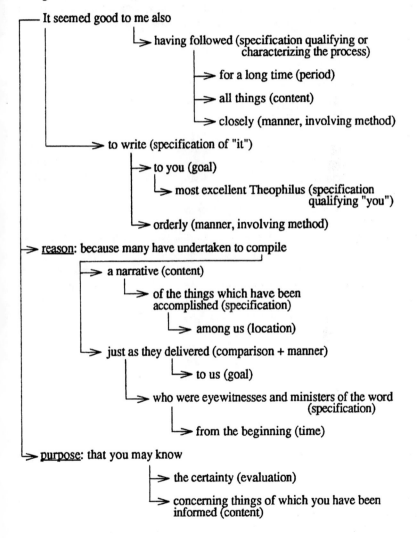

Since the information communicated in Luke 1.1-4 refers to historical events, one may also restructure the sequence of the events in order to appreciate more fully the discourse style of the author, and also to relate the historical order to the style that may be preferable in the target language. To a certain extent this will also serve as a check to ensure that the discourse pattern of the translated text is not contradicting any aspect of the actual events. On the basis, then, of the above structural outline, one may list the actual historical events in temporal order:

a   Some things happened among us
b   Original eyewitnesses and preachers told us about them
c   Many have put these in writing
d   Luke closely studied these accounts for a long time (implying that he spent considerable effort to ensure the accuracy of the material)
e   Luke then compiled an orderly report (which may suggest that his sources were not organized to his liking)
f   The result of Luke's investigations is presented to Theophilus
g   Now the facts may be accurately known.

The Greek text has the order c, a, b, since this order fits better in the reason clause. This is a stylistic device which is quite natural for Greek but rather unconventional in English if one compares the RSV reading "Inasmuch as many have undertaken to compile a narrative . . . just as they were delivered to us by those who . . ." The TEV translation followed the natural sequence of the events and introduced the reason at a later stage. This gives a more natural flow of the information: "Many people have . . . They wrote . . . And so, because . . ." The same is found in the NIV: "Many have . . . Therefore, since . . ." The New Afrikaans Version (NAV) has a similar structure. On the other hand, one may question whether the reader or hearer will appreciate the fact that Luke tried to improve on these accounts. It may be that the words "it seemed good also to me to write an orderly account" (NIV) can easily lead the reader or hearer to understand that Luke merely wanted to add another version to the reported events. The Greek text, especially the string ἄνωθεν πᾶσιν ἀκριβῶς καθεξῆς 'from the beginning everything accurately in order' seems to emphasize the motivation for Luke's decision to produce another version of the events. The TEV suggests more strongly to the reader why Luke has joined the previous reporters: "because I have carefully studied all . . . I thought it would be good to write." Note that the TEV has not rendered the Greek καί as "(to me) also" but has linked it to the reason "And so, because." This shift helps to put the emphasis on Luke's methodology, which in the Greek text is highlighted by ἄνωθεν πᾶσιν ἀκριβῶς καθεξῆς.

At this stage it is important to observe that ἄνωθεν has been rendered in the structural outline given above by "for a long time" and not by "from the beginning," which is the interpretation of most Bible translations. In Greek (during the Classical as well as the Hellenistic period) the term ἄνωθεν, when used as a time designation, does not focus upon the starting point in time, but rather on the fact that the event recorded goes back a long time. The focus is, therefore, not on what happens from a point of time in the past but on a process extending a long way back. Note that the RSV renders ἄνωθεν by "for some time past." The motivation for Luke's account of the events lies in the fact that he has spent considerable time in collecting and weighing his data. For this reason his account can be said to be more accurate and orderly. And, thus, Theophilus may have a fully reliable report.

The purpose clause at the end is especially significant as the result of its syntactic and semantic structure. Syntactically, τὴν ἀσφάλειαν 'the certainty' constitutes the grammatical object of the verb ἐπιγνῷς 'to know,' while ὧν κατηχήθης λόγων 'the things you were taught' are specified by περί 'concerning,' as being the items to which "certainty" pertains. Semantically, however, the phrase "the things you were taught" refers to the content of what is known, while "the certainty" evaluates the state of affairs with regard to a belief. Therefore, the literal expression "to know the certainty of the things you have been taught" means "to know that the things you have been taught are certainly true." The NIV has retained the literal rendering, which is undoubtedly somewhat "highbrow" if not unconventional. A reader or hearer has to pay close attention in order to really grasp the meaning.

A translator may feel that the meaning of a rendering should be quite clear if a receptor gives proper consideration to it. The translator no doubt feels this way because he has already given considerable attention to the text and has studied how the concepts have been formulated. The reader or hearer, however, has to respond immediately, and especially the hearer has little time to reflect. A rendering such as in TEV, namely, "so that you will know the full truth about everything which you have been taught," is immediately clear.

It is extremely important to realize that in no discourse is there a one-to-one obligatory link between the formal features and the semantic content which a reader must derive from the text. The translator may be convinced that the rendering decided upon after much reflection translates the source text in the best possible way. This may be true if the reader or hearer has the same frame of reference as the translator, but often a reader will interpret a rendering differently from the way in which a translator has intended, for example, the translation of the purpose clause discussed above in the New Afrikaans Version: *so kan u te wete kom dat die dinge waaroor u onderrig is, heeltemal betroubaar is.* Most readers or hearers will understand this rendering to mean "so that you will know that what you have been taught is fully reliable." That is to say, Theophilus will find that Luke's version substantiates the information he has already received from others. The purpose of Luke's gospel would then be merely to justify previous accounts and not to improve on the accuracy of the reports which, according to the structural analysis of the passage, seems to be a crucial element.

In translating a passage one must not only find suitable translational equivalents for the words of the source text (something translators have always had to do), but one must also arrange the structure of sentences within the discourse in such a way that the total discourse elicits from the reader or hearer a response which is in accord with the message of the source text. The "elements" which carry the communication are more than words and phrases. In view of the multivariant range of correspondences between syntax and semantics, the structural relations are absolutely crucial for recognizing the proper foci of the discourse. Persons who have been translators for many years are often so deeply rooted in their methodology that they seem blind to anything other than lexical correspondences. For example, during the seminars referred to in the preface of this book, some translators continued to consider even passages discussed in lectures as involving only problems of translational equivalences of individual words. This happened even directly after discussions on the necessity of paying attention to the structural pattern of the discourse. Perhaps the main reason for such conduct lies in the custom of translating a passage according to the translator's own immediate response to what is read and understood in other well-known translations used as guides. Very few translators take time to identify the principal concepts of a passage so as to determine for themselves exactly how they understand the text. Unless one properly understands (in the sense of "not misunderstanding") a passage, one cannot possibly produce a good translation. The type of outline suggested above for Luke 1.1-4 contains the elements constituting a close reading of a text. Translators are themselves readers since they have to read the source text in order to translate it. How carefully they read determines to a large extent the success of their final product.

Some people may object that mapping out each and every pericope to be translated in a way similar to what has been suggested for Luke 1.1-4 is too time consuming. But most of what has been written out in full in the above outline can be done mentally and in fact is done as part of a close reading of a text—an indispensable preliminary step before anyone can hope to translate a text correctly. A reading like that suggested above does not, however, include everything a translator should take into account, but it does include those features which are necessary for commencing the process of translating a text. That is to say, before everything else is considered, a translator must recognize the "structural flow" of the communication units of the text.

Once the translator has properly read (that is, understood) the text, the next step is to ensure, in so far as possible, that the receptors will be helped by the way in which the structural units of the translation are arranged, for these must agree with the structural conventions of the target language. In this way the reader or hearer will be helped to recognize the same foci and relationships which the translator has noticed.

By comparing the four translations given above, one can readily see that the TEV has structured the principal elements of the passage in a much better way than the other three. Once a reader knows what is at stake, the other three translations can be understood properly, but the TEV is more immediately clear. Note also how the reader is helped in the TEV by the way each new sentence is started by linking it up with what precedes. The NAV has followed the TEV to a large extent except for the final sentence which is closer to the rendering of the NIV and the RSV. Only the RSV has rendered $\check{\alpha}\nu\omega\theta\epsilon\nu$ satisfactorily by the phrase "for some time past," though the phrase "for a long time" may seem more natural to some, but this is a matter of English usage involving level of language.

It is extremely important to emphasize once more that a translator should not blindly follow another well-organized translation. Such a translation (for example, the above rendering in TEV) will surely help the translator to notice the main issues involved in communication, but one should not use the TEV as the actual source text, and thereby produce a literal translation of the TEV in the target language. The target language will probably require a structural arrangement that is significantly different from what is natural in English. What is necessary, is to determine exactly what the biblical passage is designed to communicate and then to restructure the same contents in the target language. Other translations are merely helpful guides concerning various options.

The following renderings in Zulu, Northern Sotho and Tswana illustrate how the application of the above principles and procedures has resulted in a translation that is not only overtly different in phrasing and in style, but is also much more meaningful.

The Zulu (of 1959), Northern Sotho (of 1951) and Tswana (of 1908) translations published anew in 1986/7 rendered Luke 1.1-4 as follows with due attention to the form of the Greek text resembling to a large extent the type of translation found in the RSV and NIV quoted above.

Northern Sotho

Ba bantši ba šetše ba lekile go hlomaganya taodišo ya tše di
Many have already tried to put together the report of what

diregilego mo go rena. Re di neilwe ke ba ba di bonego ka
happened here among us. It was given to us by them who saw it with

mahlo go tloga mathomong a tšona ya ba bona batseta ba yona
(their) eyes from the beginning of it, and then became the messengers of

taba yeo. Bjale ke bona ge go ntshwanetše, ge le nna ke go
this matter. Now I see that it is fitting if also I write to you about

ngwalela go hlatlamana ga tšona, wena Theofilo morategi, ke
the succession of these matters, you Theophilus beloved, and I

thomile go di latiša tšohle go tloga tlhagong ya tšona, o tle o
began to place everything consecutively from the beginning of them so

bone nnete ya ditaba tše o di rutilwego.
that you may see the truth of these matters which have been taught to you.

Zulu

Njengokuba abaningi sebezamile ukulanda ngokuhlelekile
Although many have tried to freely tell about those

ngalezozindaba ezigcwaliseké phakathi kwethu, njengalokho
matters that were fulfilled among us, just as they have given it to

basinika zona labo ababekhona kwasekuqaleni, bezibonela
us, those who have been there from the beginning and saw it

ngamehlo, beyizikhonzi zezwi, kwasengathi kuhle nakimina,
themselves, ministers of the word, it seemed also to me proper,

lokhu ngizihlolisisile zonke izinto, kusukela ekuqaleni,
since I investigated all these matters carefully, from the beginning, to

ngikulobele ngokulandelana, Theyofilu odumileyo, ukuze wazi
write to you in continuance, well-known Theophilus, so that you may know

ukuqiniseka kwalezozindaba ozifundisiweyo.
the certainty of those matters you have been taught.

Tswana

Go Motlotlegi Theofila; Ereka batho ba le bantsi ba inetse go
To the honorable sir Theophilus; since many are engaged in

kwala ka thulaganyō polèlō ea dilō tse di nañ le tlhōmamō rure
writing up matters in succession that are true to us,

mo go rona, Hèla yaka re di neilwe ke ba ba di bonyeñ ka
Just as these have been transmitted to us by those who have been

matlhō, le ba e neñ e le badihedi ba lehoko mo tshimologoñ; Le
eyewitnesses and doers of the word from the beginning; I also

nna, ka ke tlhotlhomisitse rure dilō colhe le tsa tshimologō,
since I have confirmed everything, and it from the beginning, I myself

ke nntse ke ikaeletse ha go ka nna molemō go gu kwalèla ka
intended that it would be good to write to you about the order of events so

thulaganyō, Gore u itse tlhōmamō ea dilō tse u rutilweñ mo go cōna.
that you may know the truth of the matters which you have been taught.

- - - - - - - - - - - - - - - -

The proposed translations based on the analysis pursued in the above discussion produced a text which runs as follows:

Northern Sotho

Mohlomphegi Teofilus batho ba bantši ba ngwadile ka ga ditaba
Dear Theophilus many people wrote about what happened

tše di diregilego mo lefaseng. Ba kgobokantše dilo tšeo ka
here in the land. They have collected all this

moka. Dilo tšeo ba di kwele go dihlatse tša tšona le badiredi
information. They heard it all from the witnesses and the ministers of the

ba Lentšu la Modimo go tloga mathomong. Ka lebaka leo le nna
Word of the Lord from the beginning. Therefore I also took a

ke tšere nako ye telele go di nyakišiša, ka fao ke ile ka
long time to investigate these matters, and then I

phetha go go ngwalela tšona ka tlhokomelo le ka tlhalošo ya ka
decided to write to you with care and by explaining

moo di diregilego ka gona. Ka fao o tlo kgona go hlaologanya
how it happened. Hereby you will be able to discern the full

therešo ye e tletšego ya tšona yeo o rutilwego yona.
truth of what you have been taught.

Zulu

UTeofilisi ohloniphekayo, Abantu abaningi babhale lendaba
Dear Theophilus, many people wrote the report of

yezinto ezenzeka phambi kwethu. Bayiloba njengoba siyilandiswa
what happened before (our time). They wrote it just as we were told

ngabantu kusukela ekuqaleni babengofakazi nabakhonzi bezwi.
by those who were from the beginning witnesses and ministers of the Word.

Ngalokho nami emva kokuba sengiphenyisisue konke esikhathini
Therefore, I also after having investigated everything properly

eside sengicabange kahle ngathi manginilobele ngokucophelela
for a long time thought and decided that I should write

lendaba nginilandise ngokulandelana okuyikho kwezigameko zayo.
to you and tell you of the real nature thereof.

Ngalendlela ningalazi lonke iqiniso ngezinto enazifundiswa.
Thus you will know the full truth of what you have been taught.

Tswana

Theofilo yo o tlotlegang segolo, Batho ba bantsi ba setse ba
Honorable Theophilus, Many people have already written

kwadile ka tse di dirafetseng mo go rona. Ba di kwadile fela
about what happened among us. They have written it up just as

jaaka re di neilwe ke ba ba boneng ka matlho mme ba nna
it was transmitted to us by eyewitnesses and doers of

badiredi ba lefoko go tswa kwa tshimologong. Ka jalo le nna ya
the word from the beginning. Therefore I also having

re ke sena go tlhotlhomisa tsotlhe go tswa tshimologong, ka
investigated everything from the beginning I

gopola go ka nna molemo go di go kwalela ka botlalo ka
decided to write it to you completely in proper

thulaganyo ya tsone. Ka tsela e o tle o itse boikanyego jwa
order. Thus you will know the truth of what you

mafoko a o a rutilweng.
have been taught.

In Luke 1.1-4 discussed above, one of the techniques employed was to shift the marker of the reason-clause (the first word in the Greek text) to the end of the clause so that it "introduces" the matrix. This has been done by the translations referred to above. Another important procedure is to recognize that syntactic and semantic elements do not correspond structurally. But there is a third very important factor that is crucial to the structure of a discourse, namely, clustering. And clustering is perhaps the most important element in constituting paragraphs.

Compare how the following texts (New King James Version, Revised Standard Version, New International Version, Today's English Version, Jerusalem Bible, Living Bible, New English Bible, New Afrikaans Version, and the Greek text of the United Bible Societies) divide the first part of Luke 1. The numbers indicate the verses which begin paragraph divisions in the text:

NKJ	RSV	NIV	TEV	JB	LB	NEB	NAV	UBS[1] (Grk)
5	5	5	5	5	5	5	5	5
	8	8	8	8	8	8	8	8
		11	11	11	11			
					13			
	14							
		18	18			18	18	
		19	19		19	19	19	
		21	21		21	21	21	21
		23	23	23		23		
	24						24	
					25			
	26	26	26	26	26	26	26	26

The 1986 printing of the Northern Sotho translation followed the divisions proposed by TEV while the Tswana translation divides at 5, 8 and 26.

All these texts have section headings at verses 1, 5, and 26. The Northern Sotho and Tswana texts have no headings at all. The Zulu translation has only one break at verse 5 with a heading. It also has a small paragraph sign at 8, 24 and 26 yet without indentation or additional spacing between the lines. The first four verses, which comprise the introduction to the book, include a dedication to a person named Theophilus and are syntactically constructed as one sentence in the Greek text. The second section deals with the birth of John the Baptist as foretold to his father Zechariah. It is a fairly long section (21 verses) and shows a very interesting presentation by the various translations. The New King James

----

[1] It is obvious that the editors of the Greek text paid little attention to paragraphing.

Version prints the whole section without any paragraph breaks. This is almost the same as in the UBS Greek New Testament except for a break at verse 21, where the people waiting for Zechariah are introduced. But since verses 21-23 continue to relate what happened to Zechariah, The RSV has no break at 21. The RSV breaks at 24 when Elizabeth, the wife of Zechariah, is introduced. At this point it is remarkable to notice that the NIV, TEV, JB and the NEB break at verse 23, though verse 23 relates how Zechariah returns home after his time of service. The RSV and the NAV regard verse 23 as being part of the previous section telling about what happened to Zechariah, while others link it to what happened afterwards when Zechariah returned home.

Divisions in a printed text surely influence the reader. They suggest to the reader that what follows involves a new event or episode which may be considered apart from others. As such, the break at verse 14 in the RSV is remarkable, since at verse 13 the angel begins to speak to Zechariah and continues up to the end of verse 17. This break in the RSV suggests that the first sentence of the angel's message may be considered as an introduction or, perhaps more likely, as the gist of the message, while from verse 14 and onward detailed events are recorded. This break at verse 14 becomes even more remarkable if one considers that the angel is introduced at verse 11 without any break in the RSV. The LB introduces a break at verse 11 as well as at verse 13, grouping Zechariah's experience in the sanctuary as a unit, followed by the message of the angel as another unit. This is repeated at 18 and 19, so that the events directly related to Zechariah are clearly set off from the events recorded in reference to the angel. The LB generally has more paragraph breaks than most other translations, and these breaks surely facilitate the reading. However, it is remarkable that the LB has no break at either 23 or 24, which may be more fitting than its break at 25.

The JB has a break at verse 11 when the angel is introduced, but this section continues up to verse 23, while at the end of verse 20 the angel's part in the narrative ends and the people waiting for Zechariah are introduced. As such, the JB suggests to the reader that verses 11 through 22 are a unit dealing with Zechariah's experience in the sanctuary. Zechariah thus becomes the focus of the passage. This is reinforced by printing verses 23 through 25 as another unit which reports Zechariah's return to his home and what happened to his wife. By printing the text with a break at verse 24 as in the case of the RSV and the NAV, Elizabeth is given somewhat more prominence.

Some people may object that these breaks are not that important, but if one reads these various translations simultaneously it becomes clear how the reader is almost directed to highlight the different sections of the narrative in distinctly different ways. Focus is an important feature of any narrative and certainly conditions a reader's reactions to what is communicated. The effect may seem slight, and often even hardly noticeable, yet one cannot deny that these indicators in a text (being essentially semiotic signs) condition the reader's understanding of the narrative. This becomes even more apparent when a text is heard being read. The way the reader pauses or changes the tone of voice has considerable effect on the receptor. Texts were made of receptors listening to a variety of readers, and the results showed that when a text was read with a continuous flow without any breaks, the receptors found the narrative dull. On the other hand, a reading with proper breaks made the story come to life. Furthermore, the spacing of the breaks conditioned the hearers in their response to the central theme of the communication. In one of these tests a story about an incident between two people was read so differently by two different persons (who read aloud while others listened) that the sympathy of one audience toward the people in the text was completely different from that of the other audience.

The reasons for these distinctively different reactions can be attributed to the different semiotic signs that are utilized by the receptors to build up a frame of reference. In fact, one's frame of reference is perhaps one of the most important factors involved in understanding or misunderstanding a message.

It may also be important for a translator to study the general social conventions of a particular community as well as the patterns of their language in order to determine how these receptors usually cluster information. A local newspaper in my area recently decided not to have their paragraphs exceed four full sentences, and if three or four sentences were required they should not be long sentences. The publishers came to this conclusion after having surveyed the reactions of their readers to certain reports in their paper. It seemed that if a paragraph was too long, most readers lost courage, as it were, and tended to ignore important elements of information. By carefully planning the clustering of the information which they wanted their readers to appreciate, they believed they could greatly influence the understanding of their readers.

In translating Luke 1.5-25 about the manner in which the birth of John the Baptist was foretold, one has to recognize that the text has four main units. The first involves a setting of the stage by giving (a) personal information about the protagonists, namely, Zechariah and his wife Elizabeth (verses 5-7), and (b) data on how Zechariah had to perform a certain task in the temple on a particular occasion (8-10). This second part of the setting also introduces certain passive actors, namely, the people who had come to worship in the temple. Having spelled out the setting (5-10), the author then narrates the events leading up to the birth of John by introducing three essential episodes. The first (11-20) tells how an angel appeared to Zechariah and what the two talked about. This conversation has three subdivisions: the angel speaking (13-17), Zechariah responding (18), and the angel speaking again (19-20). The second episode (21-22) portrays Zechariah and the people. The first episode has an introduction (11-12) and the second episode has a closing (23). The final episode (24-25) introduces Elizabeth who makes the message of the angel come true.

The text, therefore, seems to suggest the following basic units:

A. 5-10   :   <u>setting</u>
    > 5-7   :   Zechariah and Elizabeth
    > 8-10   :   Zechariah and the people
B. 11-20   :   <u>Zechariah and the angel</u>
    > 11-12 :   introduction
    > 13-17 :   angel speaking
    > 18   :   Zechariah speaking
    > 19-20 :   angel speaking
C. 21-22   :   <u>Zechariah and the people</u>
    > 23   :   closing
D. 24-25   :   <u>Elizabeth</u>

Note how the TEV has printed the text. The verse numbers 5, 8, 11, 18, 19, 21 and 23 are bigger than the rest, for these verses are also indented to indicate new paragraphs. The NIV has done the same. The RSV has gone even further by printing part of the angel's message in poetic form, though there is hardly anything in the source text to suggest this.

There is certainly more than one way to cluster the text and to arrange the layout of the printed text. The following is merely a suggestion of how one can present the text of the TEV while introducing an additional break at verse 24. At this stage too little research[2] has been done to be prescriptive about how paragraphing should be carried out so as to reflect different degrees of structural breaks. What is suggested here should rather be seen as a way of introducing the problem for discussion.

---

2 A seminar on <u>Style, Format and the Reader</u> (1988) led to the preparation of a forthcoming book which will provide insights on this important topic.

The Birth of John the Baptist is Announced

5   During the time when Herod was king of Judaea, there was a priest named Zechariah, who belonged to the priestly order of Abijah. His wife's name was Elizabeth; she also belonged to a priestly family. 6They both lived good lives in God's sight and obeyed fully all the Lord's laws and commands. 7They had no children because Elizabeth could not have any, and she and Zechariah were both very old.

8   One day Zechariah was doing his work as a priest in the Temple, taking his turn in the daily service. 9According to the custom followed by the priests, he was chosen by lot to burn incense on the altar. So he went into the Temple of the Lord 10while the crowd of people outside prayed during the hour when the incense was burnt.

11   An angel of the Lord appeared to him, standing on the right of the altar where the incense was burnt. 12When Zechariah saw him, he was alarmed and felt afraid. 13But the angel said to him, "Don't be afraid, Zechariah! God has heard your prayer, and your wife Elizabeth will bear a son. You are to name him John. 14How glad and happy you will be and many others will be when he is born! 15He will be a great man in the Lord's sight. He must not drink any wine or strong drink. From his very birth he will be filled with the Holy Spirit, 16and he will bring back many of the people of Israel to the Lord their God. 17He will go ahead of the Lord, strong and mighty like the prophet Elijah. He will bring fathers and children together again; he will turn disobedient people back to the way of thinking of the righteous; he will get the Lord's people ready for him."

18   Zechariah said to the angel, "How shall I know if this is so? I am an old man and my wife is old also."

19   "I am Gabriel," the angel answered. "I stand in the presence of God, who sent me to speak to you and tell you this good news. 20But you have not believed my message, which will come true at the right time. Because you have not believed, you will be unable to speak, you will remain silent until the day my promise to you comes true."

21   In the meantime the people were waiting for Zechariah and wondering why he was spending such a long time in the Temple. 22When he came out, he could not speak to them, and so they knew that he had seen a vision in the Temple. Unable to say a word, he made signs to them with his hands.

23   When his period of service in the Temple was over, Zechariah went back home.

24   Some time later his wife Elizabeth became pregnant and did not leave the house for five months. 25"Now at last the Lord has helped me," she said. "He has taken away my public disgrace!"

Chapter 5

A Receptor's Understanding of
a Reasoned Discourse: Romans 8.1-17

Johannes P. Louw

Though Romans 8.1-17 and Luke 1.1-25 (discussed in chapter 4) have several features in common, the flow of argument in Romans 8.1-17 differs greatly in complexity from that of the narrative in Luke 1.1-25. This is especially true in the rhetorical aspects of the two discourses. A passage such as Romans 8.1-17 is more tightly woven syntactically and contains a number of stylistic subtleties which are employed to highlight the relationship between the constituents of the discourse. Relations such as topic, comment, reason, result, condition, concession, specification, purpose, linkage, equivalence, means, dependency, manner, etc. function to a much larger extent in reasoned than in narrative discourse. This is why reasoned discourse is often more difficult for hearers or readers to follow. Misunderstanding, therefore, also has a higher rate of probability. The style involves more nominalizations which alone are less specific and therefore require more decoding by the hearer or reader before the possible intention of the text can be grasped. A translator has to be more careful to avoid misunderstanding.

Another important aspect is that reasoned discourse seems to contain more discrepancies between syntactic and semantic structures. This involves the age-old problem of the relation between form and meaning. Thus, it becomes imperative to begin by mapping the form of the text in such a way as to highlight the syntactic relations between the constituent parts. These relations constitute the basic elements of the semantic interpretation.

Before attempting to translate Romans 8.1-17 it is almost always necessary to map the syntactic structure of the discourse. But, why 1-17? How do we know that verses 1-17 should be analyzed as a larger unit? The answer is simply: we do not know before we have analyzed the total text. To determine which sections form a unit, one must see how the constituent parts fit together. As a working hypothesis one can begin with sections traditionally marked as constituting a paragraph or pericope. Once a fairly large stretch of language is analyzed, it soon becomes apparent which units are linked more closely together. By following these indicators, one can either validate the hypothesis or change to a different grouping of the material. By checking and rechecking one can finally arrive at a decision where to begin and end a section. Therefore, marking off a particular section as a unit is the result of one's analysis.

To understand Paul's reasoning in Romans 8.1-17, the first step is to map the syntactic constructions of the source text. The following outline of the syntactic structure of the Greek text of Romans 8.1-17, employing a very literal rendering in English, may now be considered.

There is, however, an initial question to be decided before one can map the very first sentence, since the function of γάρ 'for' at the beginning of verse 2 must be determined. Is it a marker of cause or reason between events, or is it merely a discourse marker introducing a new sentence or paragraph? It seems quite plausible that γάρ links κατάκριμα 'condemnation' with ἠλευθέρωσεν 'set free' and accordingly marks a reason relation: "there is no condemnation because there is a setting free." On the other hand, a close scrutiny of Paul's style shows that Paul often (as in verses 3, 5, 6, etc.) employs this lexical meaning of γάρ in a way similar to the use of γάρ as a discourse marker. This happens generally when a reason is elaborated into a new thought unit. As such, γάρ lexically expresses the semantic notion of reason, while it also functions stylistically as a discourse marker. This is a peculiarity of Pauline style. One can, therefore, analyze the first four verses of Romans 8 as one unitary sentence construction. The whole stretch from γάρ in verse 2 up to the end of verse 4 (or even further) can be embedded syntactically as reason units qualifying κατάκριμα. This is, strictly speaking, one syntactic string. But, what is more, the section marked as verse 3 contains an anakolouthon that may be solved by recognizing an ellipsis (see analysis below).

On the other hand, in view of the discourse style one can also analyze the γάρ-sections as units in themselves, with γάρ marking the beginning of these units. Nevertheless, these units will have to be understood semantically as reasons explaining verse 1, which would then be semantically a title heading. The phrase ἄρα νῦν 'therefore now' in verse 1 links with what precedes. And if one considers the total argument of Paul's reasoning from the very beginning of the discourse, it becomes apparent that the semantic content of verse 1 echoes a basic contention in the Letter to the Romans, namely, δικαιοσύνη ἐκ πίστεως 'being put right with God through faith.' From the beginning of chapter 5, Paul has already touched upon this theme occasionally by showing that faith involves receiving what Christ has done to set people free.

On this basis one may analyze the first four verses as a unit involving four sets of constructions. The numbers in the left margin refer to the traditional verse divisions, while the other numbers with their sub-divisions (.1, .2, .3, etc.) indicate the structural strings. Note that verse 4 coincides with the syntactic unit 4.6-4.10:

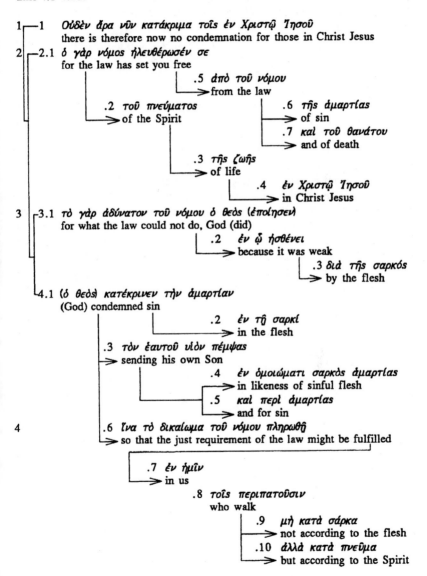

1—1 *Οὐδὲν ἄρα νῦν κατάκριμα τοῖς ἐν Χριστῷ Ἰησοῦ*
there is therefore now no condemnation for those in Christ Jesus

2 ⌐2.1 *ὁ γὰρ νόμος ἠλευθέρωσέν σε*
for the law has set you free

.5 *ἀπὸ τοῦ νόμου*
→ from the law

.2 *τοῦ πνεύματος*
→ of the Spirit

.6 *τῆς ἁμαρτίας*
→ of sin

.7 *καὶ τοῦ θανάτου*
→ and of death

.3 *τῆς ζωῆς*
→ of life

.4 *ἐν Χριστῷ Ἰησοῦ*
→ in Christ Jesus

3 ⌐3.1 *τὸ γὰρ ἀδύνατον τοῦ νόμου ὁ θεὸς (ἐποίησεν)*
for what the law could not do, God (did)

.2 *ἐν ᾧ ἠσθένει*
→ because it was weak

.3 *διὰ τῆς σαρκός*
→ by the flesh

4.1 *(ὁ θεὸς) κατέκρινεν τὴν ἁμαρτίαν*
(God) condemned sin

.2 *ἐν τῇ σαρκί*
→ in the flesh

.3 *τὸν ἑαυτοῦ υἱὸν πέμψας*
→ sending his own Son

.4 *ἐν ὁμοιώματι σαρκὸς ἁμαρτίας*
→ in likeness of sinful flesh

.5 *καὶ περὶ ἁμαρτίας*
→ and for sin

4 .6 *ἵνα τὸ δικαίωμα τοῦ νόμου πληρωθῇ*
→ so that the just requirement of the law might be fulfilled

.7 *ἐν ἡμῖν*
→ in us

.8 *τοῖς περιπατοῦσιν*
who walk

.9 *μὴ κατὰ σάρκα*
→ not according to the flesh

.10 *ἀλλὰ κατὰ πνεῦμα*
→ but according to the Spirit

From the above outline it is apparent that the discourse is built up by means of a number of fairly short phrase units with specific elements marking the relations between the units. These elements will, in the end, prove to be the crucial semantic markers that determine the understanding of what is communicated. For example, in 2.1 there are two sets of phrase units enlarging respectively upon either νόμος 'law' or ἠλευθέρωσεν 'set free.' Those units enlarging upon *law*, namely, *of the Spirit*, *of life* and *in Christ Jesus* follow one upon another in sequence by which the second qualifies the first, while the third qualifies the second. That is to say, 2.2 tells us *what* law is at stake, namely, the law *of the Spirit*. The relation between *law* and *Spirit* is marked in Greek by the genitive case represented in the English translation by *of*.

The crucial question is how the expression *the law of the Spirit* is to be understood. Does it mean *the law about the Spirit* or *the law which the Spirit gives* or *the spiritual law*? Similarly, one must explain 2.3 "the Spirit of life." Again the genitive construction is rendered in English by *of*. What is the meaning? Is it *the living Spirit* or *the Spirit that gives life* or *life's spirit*, that is, the spirit that life gives? And in 2.4 one must account for the relation expressed by ἐν 'in.' Note also how ἠλευθέρωσεν 'set free' is marked by 2.5, a prepositional phrase introduced by ἀπό 'from,' and two (2.6 and 2.7) genitive constructions "of sin" and "of death." Questions such as these need to be clearly answered before one can even venture to translate the passage. Answers to these questions will also help to determine what the term *law* refers to, and, likewise, how πνεῦμα is to be understood, as "Spirit" or "spirit." Similarly, one must also determine what *life* refers to: is it merely biological existence, or is it the distinctive quality of Christian life which leads on to eternal life? If one translates "for the law of the Spirit of life in Christ Jesus has set you free from the law of sin and death," one has only substituted English words for the Greek so that for the reader or hearer what is said is still more or less Greek.

The NIV has left everything "Greek" except for 2.4 ("*in* Christ Jesus") by translating "because through Christ Jesus the law of the Spirit of life set me free from the law of sin and death." The TEV reflects how the translators understood 2.3 and 2.4 by rendering the Greek as "for the law of the Spirit, which brings us life in union with Christ Jesus, has set me free from the law of sin and death." The NEB reads "because in Christ Jesus the life-giving law of the Spirit has set you free from the law of sin and death."

From the point of view of the reader or hearer, the differences between the translations quoted above are very important, since the reader or hearer generally does not have the trained insight of a scholar and has to interpret the translated text at face value in order to come to some understanding of the message. It is, therefore, important (perhaps the most important requirement) to help the reader or hearer to make the "correct" interpretation on the basis of the translated text or, at least, to ensure in so far as possible that no misunderstanding will result from the way in which a translation is phrased. Again, this shows how important it is to ask: for whom am I translating? Translating is not merely reproducing the text in another language, as we so often tend to say. It is essentially telling the reader or hearer of another language what message is conveyed by the source text. Therefore, translating without a receptor in mind has no purpose. To produce a new translation of the Bible by focusing only on the text and its structure in order to reproduce the source text as faithfully as possible may sound commendable, but if the receptor becomes lost in the process, the whole undertaking is futile.

The three translations quoted above have been attempts at dealing with the relations involved, but at no time was sufficient attention paid to the manner in which the receptor might understand (or rather misunderstand) the term *law*. Are "the law of the Spirit" and "the law of sin and death" particular judicial codes? In other words, does *law* refer to a codified set of regulations? How will the reader or hearer in Africa, for example, respond to a term which may be used as a translational equivalent of *law*? In verse 3 the term *law* appears to refer to the Jewish law, or more explicitly, the Mosaic law. This can easily be taken to be the meaning of *law* in "the law of sin and death" in the sense of the Law that tells us about or leads to sin and its result, namely, death. A number of modern translators understand *law* in this sense. However, there are some who take the word in the wider sense of pertaining to law in general. But the argument expounded in the previous chapters of the Letter to the Romans seems to indicate that the author had the Jewish Law in mind. The controversy which Paul deals with is the question of how far the Christians in Rome should submit to the requirements of the Jewish Law in order to be God's people. This was the main point of contention between Jewish Christians and Gentile Christians in the early stages of Christianity. This problem is also dealt with explicitly in other letters of Paul, for example, Galatians and Corinthians. Finally, for a person with Paul's background and education it seems unlikely that *law* can refer to anything else than the Mosaic Law.

But what then is "the law of the Spirit"? Is it likewise another judicial code? Or is it a phrase used by Paul for the sake of rhetorical effect to balance the syntax of the sentence? As such, the expression "the law of the Spirit" refers to the control which the Spirit exercises in the life of the believer as opposed to the control exercised by the Law. If this is the meaning of the total expression, πνεῦμα must then be understood as "Spirit," i.e., the Holy Spirit, and not as "spirit." The contrast, therefore, seems to be between the governing force of either the Spirit or the Law in the lives of people. The will of the Spirit became a law, so to speak, for the Christian believers. For the Jews the Mosaic Law was the most important factor controlling their behavior. In the beginning of the Letter to the Romans, Paul occasionally discusses the value and position of the Law. He explicitly argues that it is not the Law which brings people into a right relationship with God. The Law is an instructor (see Romans, chapters 2 and 3) teaching what sin is. It is faith, however, that puts people in a right relationship to God. In Romans 8.2 the same idea is expressed in a more concise way. This makes verse 1 a summary statement in reference to the preceding chapters as well as an introduction to what follows. The γάρ clauses now clearly become motivations for the recapitulation of the former arguments.

With all this in mind the translator must determine how to render Romans 8.1-4 in such a way that the reader or hearer will be able to follow the development of these complex relations. We may now return to the outline of the Greek text given above by trying to formulate the relations, meanings, and references in such a way that a receptor can really understand what Paul is saying. This can only be done when the translator properly understands the message. Apart from everything that has been said above, a translation is nothing else than a translator telling the readers or hearers how the translator has read and understood the passage. The more obscure a translation is, the more we can be certain that the translator was not really sure what the source text meant.

Let us assume for the sake of explaining the appropriate methodology that the translator (or rather the translation committee or team) has studied all the relevant commentaries and has decided, on the basis of the above mapping of the structural units of Romans 8.1-4, that there are four structural strings, of which the first is the main statement serving as a heading or title. This title is in turn explained by the second string (2.1-2.4), giving the reason why the main statement is valid. The following sections, 3.1-3.3 and 4.1-4.10, are further elaborations explaining 2.1-2.4 more fully. This is also in line with Pauline style in general.

The next step should be to determine and formulate the meaning expressed by the various markers of relations, especially the prepositions and the declensional case endings. The first one occurs in the structural string marked as 1. The ancient Greek grammarians referred to a complete single syntactic construction as a colon (κῶλον) and from now on we may refer to 1, 2 (that is, the total of 2.1-2.4) as colons or cola. For a fuller treatment of the theoretical basis of colons, see J.P. Louw, *Semantics of New Testament Greek* (Fortress Press, 1982), chapters 9 and 10.

In colon 1 the preposition έν 'in' marks a relation of close personal association. In English one can render this meaning by phrases such as "one with, in union with, joined closely to," etc. The TEV translation renders this meaning quite appropriately by "There is no condemnation now for those who live in union with Christ Jesus." In some languages it may be preferable to employ a verb rather than a noun like *condemnation*, since the semantic class of *condemnation* is event. During the practical sessions of the seminar mentioned in the preface to this book, it was suggested that for some of the African languages it would be more natural and less open to misunderstanding to render colon 1 as "Those who live in union with Christ Jesus are no longer condemned" or ". . . will not be condemned." Since κατάκριμα 'condemnation' in Romans 8.1 implies "punishment," some translators decided that for their readers or hearers a term closer to the notion of punishment will be more meaningful in order to understand fully what Paul is saying. Therefore, they suggested translating "Therefore there is now no punishment for those who . . ." or "Therefore those who live in close fellowship with Christ Jesus will not be punished."

In line with the above discussions on the phrases "law of the Spirit" and "law of sin and death" we may now consider the various relations between the constituent units of colon 2. The main contrast is between two forces governing the lives of people. The one pertains to control by the Holy Spirit and the other to control by the Jewish Law. The Spirit is related to life, and the Law is related to sin which brings death. The life which the Spirit gives comes from the close fellowship with Christ Jesus. A possible way of rendering these relations with a view to the reader's or hearer's comprehension may be as follows: "For the Holy Spirit who gives us real life when we live in close fellowship with Christ Jesus has become to us like a law that sets us free from the law that tells us about sin that results in death." Note how καί 'and' linking "sin" and "death" is not to be understood as a marker of addition, but is to be taken in its other meaning of sequence, namely, "sin" and then "death."

Colon 2 is semantically very complex and because of the compact syntactic phrasing of the source text, it is difficult, if not impossible, to translate without making explicit what is implicitly marked by the grammatical cases and the accompanying prepositions.

Many translators may feel that the rendering suggested above is far more a paraphrase than a translation. Yet, translation and paraphrase are but two aspects of the same process. This has been well argued by E.H. Glassman in *The Translation Debate* (Intervarsity Press, Downers Grove, IL, 1981). In fact, any rendering involves saying in another language what is understood to be the message of the source text. What many people call a paraphrase is merely a translation which makes more implicit information explicit. Judgments about translation versus paraphrase depend largely on the grid of comparison which is employed. All translations, even so-called conservative translations, include "paraphrases." What is important is not primarily how a translation is phrased but whether anything is added, distorted, or left out of the source text. A translator must decide how much of the implicit information should go into the translated text and how much can be left implicit or referred to footnotes. It all depends on the receptors for whom a translation is made. Some do not favor footnotes at all. If receptors are willing to accept footnotes, a translation may be closer to the form of the original. This may enable the reader or hearer to experience something of the style, imagery, and discourse structure of the original. Footnotes, then, are necessary to help the receptor not to misunderstand the message. Whatever choice a translator makes, it nevertheless remains essential for the personal use of the translator to phrase the meaning of the source text in a way similar to that suggested above. In this way the translator can make certain his or her precise understanding of the intent of the source text. Once this is established, a translator can more meaningfully decide what type of rendering best suits the needs of the receptors. It is definitely wrong to follow a procedure favored by some translators who simply copy a well-known and respected English translation more or less literally. This usually means completely ignoring the hearers or readers for whom the translation is supposed to be "the Bible in their own language."

The next two colons clearly illustrate the argument developed in the preceding paragraphs. The NIV has opted to present receptors (who would like to have a close formal correspondence translation) with a rendering that presupposes a fair knowledge of the content, argument, and style of presentation of Paul's letters:

> For what the law was powerless to do in that it was weakened by the sinful nature,[a] God did by sending his own Son in the likeness of sinful man to be a sin offering.[b] And so he condemned sin in sinful man, in order that the righteous requirements of the law might be fully met in us, who do not live according to the sinful nature but according to the Spirit.

Footnote a states that the expression "sinful nature" occurring twice in the translated text renders a Greek term more often translated by "flesh," and footnote b indicates that the phrase "to be a sin offering" represents the Greek expression more literally translated as "for sin." Both the text of the translation and the footnotes show the concern for a formal correspondence translation. Such a translation does, of course, serve a purpose in affording the reader (though hardly the hearer) with an English "print out" of the original so that the reader may interpret the intent of the text on the basis of his own knowledge and insight rather than have the advantage of a more thorough reproduction of the message of the source text. Translations of this kind are favored by persons who wish to know how the syntax of the source text is structured. But such a translation should be compared with one having its focus on the meaning of the source text. Having both types of translations is helpful, but to rely on a formal type of translation alone is to risk misunderstanding, unless the receptor knows the message beforehand and is therefore mainly interested in how the message is conveyed, not in what is conveyed. This again shows how important it is to translate for a specific audience. Translation is not an activity in and of itself; it is a service to readers or hearers.

Colons 3 and 4 of our passage are introduced by γάρ 'for' which suggests that what follows is an explanation, or perhaps a motivation, for what has been said in colon 2. Nevertheless, one cannot deny that the source text is somewhat overly elaborate in its formulation and therefore not at all easy to follow, but it is typical of the condensed nature of Pauline style. A detailed analysis of the constituent units of these two colons may help the translator account for the manner in which the content is or should be understood. This may then serve to determine the communicative value of the NIV quoted in comparison with other translations.

In colons 2-4 the terms νόμος 'Law,' πνεῦμα 'Spirit,' and σάρξ 'flesh' are consistently foregrounded. In colons 3 and 4 σάρξ is closely linked to sin and to why people cannot in themselves comply with what the Law requires. In colon 3.1-3.3 we have an interesting case of the relation between syntax and semantics: τὸ ἀδύνατον τοῦ νόμου, literally, "the disability of the Law," seems at first sight to be linked with κατέκρινεν 'he condemned,' though τὴν ἁμαρτίαν 'sin' should more naturally be taken as the syntactic "object" following κατέκρινεν. The construction is syntactically condensed and it seems preferable to recognize an ellipsis by introducing something like ἐποίησεν 'he did.' Many translations follow this procedure, which entails linking ἀδύνατον semantically to σάρξ 'flesh' although it is syntactically linked to νόμος. This solution is suggested by the prepositions ἐν 'in' and διά 'on account of' in 3.2 and 3.3, both of which denote the reason for ἀδύνατον 'impossible.' That is to say, νόμος 'law' is semantically not the experiencer of the disability, but human nature is.

Colon 3 indicates that because human nature is weak it does not have the ability to comply with the law. Because of this incapacity, God came to the rescue. The phrase "the disability of the Law" does not mean that the Law is lacking in strength, but rather that the lack of strength pertains to complying with the Law. Grammatically a genitive such as τοῦ νόμου 'of the Law' in this context is called an "objective genitive" which in case grammar would be called "the affected."

Colon 4 explains how God came to the rescue by condemning sin in human nature. The prepositional construction in 4.2 marks the area in which sin operates. Colon 4.3 then states the manner in which God came to the rescue, that is, "by sending his Son." The two prepositional phrases introduced by $\dot{\epsilon}\nu$ 'in' and $\pi\epsilon\rho\acute{\iota}$ 'for, concerning' mark the state in which his Son was sent, namely, in the likeness of human nature, and they specify the topic involved, namely, "with regard to sin," implying that his Son had to deal with the factor of sin. Though not explicitly stated in this context, the way in which Christ dealt with sin is known from other passages of Scripture, namely, by giving himself as a sin offering, that is, as a sacrifice. Note how the NIV, though primarily a formal correspondence translation, has introduced this reference into the text. This also shows how paraphrase and translation are aspects of the same process.

Colon 4.6 (coinciding with verse 4 of the traditional text divisions) now follows upon $\kappa\alpha\tau\acute{\epsilon}\kappa\rho\iota\nu\epsilon\nu$ 'he condemned' as the intended result, namely, that the requirements of the Law, which human nature could not fulfill because of its inherent weakness, may be complied with in our case (4.7), since we are people who live (the figurative extension of meaning of "to walk") in accordance with what the Holy Spirit does in these matters (see colon 2) and not in accordance with what our human nature does.

We may now summarize the above analysis by spelling out the semantic content of colons 3 and 4. This can then be a guide in producing a fully meaningful translation. Colons 3 and 4 are simply an explanation of how we are set free from sin and enjoy real life given by the Spirit when we live in close union with Christ; we are not set free because we comply with the requirements of the Law. In fact, our human nature lacks the capacity to comply with the Law. However, what we cannot do, God does, because he has condemned sin (not us) by sending his Son and having him fully identify with us, so that his Son may deal with our sins by being a sacrifice for them. Since God has come to our rescue, we can now be said to have complied with the requirements of the Law, not because of what our human nature has accomplished, but because we live in accordance with what the Holy Spirit has brought about in our lives.

Now that we understand the meaning of the passage in detail, we can return to the NIV translation and determine how in a second reading of the text the previously rather obscure rendering seems to be much more intelligible. This can also be done with other translations, even including the dynamic equivalent translation of the TEV.

An analysis of the following portion of Romans 8.1-17 will demonstrate how the entire section can be outlined on the basis of 25 colon structures. The numbers to the left of the linking lines refer to the traditional verse numbers:

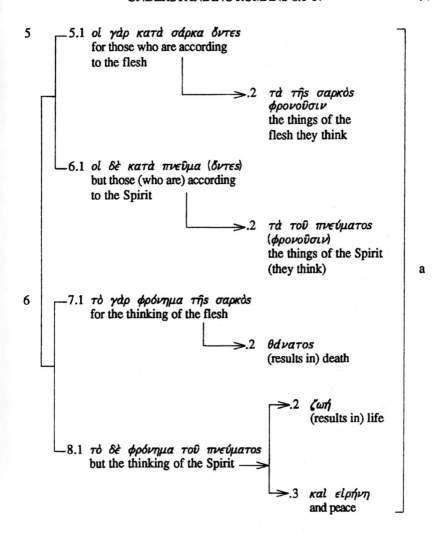

Colons 7 and 8 comprise the result of what is stated in colons 5 and 6 by taking up the opposition between flesh (human nature) and Spirit. Colons 5-8 are, in fact, a restatement of what has been said in colon 2 on the basis of the explanation given to colon 2 in colons 3 and 4.

The following sub-section (colons 9-13) is a further restatement of the "flesh-Spirit" opposition:

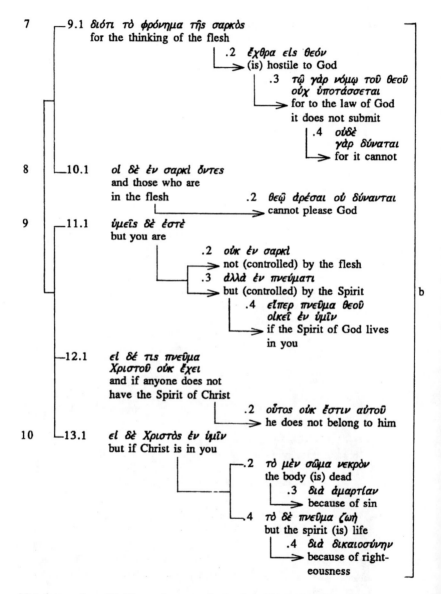

Note how colons 11-13 merely expand what is said in colons 9 and 10.

Colons 14-17 take the flesh-Spirit opposition a little further:

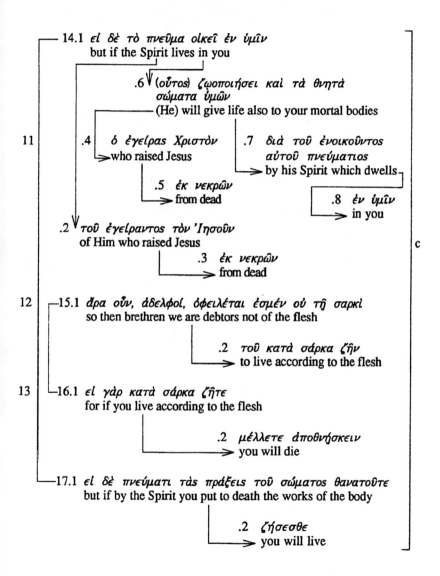

The three subsections a, b, and c (colons 5-8, 9-13, and 14-17) exhibit a typical feature of Pauline style, namely, repetition of the same basic concept from different perspectives and with different foci. Therefore, these subsections are merely elaborate expansions of what has been said in colons 1-4. We may now designate the overall structure as:

A: colons 1-4
B: colons 5-17 comprising three subsections,
    a (colons 5-8), b (colons 9-13), and c (colons 14-17).

Note how cluster a (5-8) is parallel in structure: flesh- Spirit (5-6) and flesh-Spirit (7-8). The basic meaning is: control by sinful human nature brings about death, and the control by the Spirit brings life and peace. Cluster b (9-13) is again parallel in that 9-10 focuses on human nature, while 11-13 focuses on the Spirit. In cluster c (14-17) the work of the Spirit, stated in 11-13, is extended to God the Father and is repeated in colon 17. Colons 14 and 17 deal with the Spirit, while colons 15 and 16 contrast the work of human nature. The parallel structures of clusters a and b are now changed to a chiastic arrangement: Spirit-flesh-flesh-Spirit. The content of cluster c (14-17) is a repetition of the basic concept of clusters a and b.

Finally, colons 18-25 link to 5-17 in that they continue the basic theme, though focusing only on the work of the Spirit:

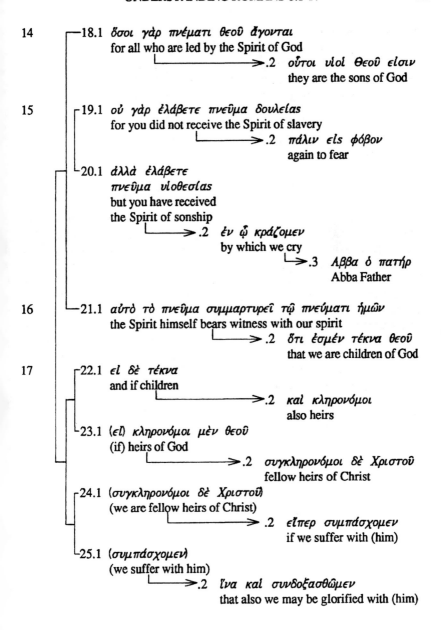

14   18.1 ὅσοι γὰρ πνέματι θεοῦ ἄγονται
          for all who are led by the Spirit of God
                                        .2 οὗτοι υἱοί θεοῦ εἰσιν
                                            they are the sons of God

15   19.1 οὐ γὰρ ἐλάβετε πνεῦμα δουλείας
          for you did not receive the Spirit of slavery
                                        .2 πάλιν εἰς φόβον
                                            again to fear

     20.1 ἀλλὰ ἐλάβετε
          πνεῦμα υἱοθεσίας
          but you have received
          the Spirit of sonship
                                .2 ἐν ᾧ κράζομεν
                                    by which we cry
                                        .3 Αββα ὁ πατήρ
                                            Abba Father

16   21.1 αὐτὸ τὸ πνεῦμα συμμαρτυρεῖ τῷ πνεύματι ἡμῶν
          the Spirit himself bears witness with our spirit
                                        .2 ὅτι ἐσμέν τέκνα θεοῦ
                                            that we are children of God

17   22.1 εἰ δὲ τέκνα
          and if children
                                        .2 καὶ κληρονόμοι
                                            also heirs

     23.1 (εἰ) κληρονόμοι μὲν θεοῦ
          (if) heirs of God
                                        .2 συγκληρονόμοι δὲ Χριστοῦ
                                            fellow heirs of Christ

     24.1 (συγκληρονόμοι δὲ Χριστοῦ)
          (we are fellow heirs of Christ)
                                        .2 εἴπερ συμπάσχομεν
                                            if we suffer with (him)

     25.1 (συμπάσχομεν)
          (we suffer with him)
                                .2 ἵνα καὶ συνδοξασθῶμεν
                                    that also we may be glorified with (him)

Colon 18 is repeated in 21 with 19 and 20 commenting on 18 and 21 by means of contrast. This constitutes a ring-composition, highlighting the various items. What is said in 18-21 prepares the way for the conclusion stated in colons 22-25: a slave has no rights, but a child has, especially an inheritance.

The structural pattern may now be summarized as follows:

A: colons 1-4
B: colons 5-17 (involving 5-8, 9-13, 14-17 as three subclusters)
C: colons 18-25.

This structural outline based on the relations between the constituent units may now be reflected in the paragraphing of the translated text of Romans 8.1-17. Incidentally, the verse divisions of Romans 8.1-17 parallel the main clusters, though this should not be an obstacle in sections where it does not coincide as readily as in Romans 8.1-17. It is important to relate the traditional verse divisions to the pattern of the text and not to pattern the text according to the verse divisions. Verse divisions should not have a prominent place in a translation. Rather, the determining factor should be paragraphing according to the structural features of a text. In Romans 8.1-17 one would think that the paragraphing should be fairly obvious, but if we compare the following chart with the structural analysis discussed above, it is obvious how these translations (King James, New King James, Revised Standard Version, New International Version, Today's English Version, Jerusalem Bible, New English Bible, and the Greek text of the United Bible Societies) differ in this respect. The numbers refer to the traditional verse numbers:

	KJ	NKJ	RSV	NIV	TEV	JB	NEB	UBS (Greek)
A: 1-4	1-17	1-11	1-8	1-4	1-8	1-4	1-4	1-11
B: a 5-6				5-8		5-11	5-8	
b 7-10			9-11	9-11	9-11		9-11	
c 11-13		12-17	12-17	12-17	12-17	12-13	12-13	12-17
C: 14-17						14-17	14-17	

The New King James (Revised Authorized Version) has two divisions (as in the UBS Greek text) titled as "Free from Indwelling Sin" and "Sonship Through the Spirit."

Though it is possible to justify a somewhat different analysis of the paragraph structure of Romans 8.1-17, it seems obvious that in most cases little attention seems to have been given to paragraphing according to a careful analysis of the text. The Zulu translation (of 1959), the Tswana (of 1908) and the Northern Sotho (of 1951) in their 1986/7 printings show a similar tendency. The Zulu has only a minor break indicated by a small paragraph marker at verse 12 while the Tswana has a major break at 12. The Northern Sotho has two breaks at verses 9 and 12. Readers, however, are often guided to a considerable extent by the divisions and subdivisions of a text. Accordingly, much more attention should be given to this aspect of translating. Research into this matter is presently in progress and, hopefully, will be the subject of a further volume in this monograph series.

The following extracts of proposed new translations in Zulu, Northern Sotho and Tswana based on the analysis of Rom 8.2-4 in the outline discussed above and the discussions at the workshop may be considered. In each case the present translation is given first and followed by the new proposal.

Northern Sotho

Gobane molao wa Moya wa go phela ka Kriste Jesu o nkhunolotše
For the law of the Spirit to live through Christ Jesus freed me from

molaong wa sebe le wa lehu. Gobane se se šitilego Molao ke ge
the law of sin and death. For what made the law powerless is that

o fokodišwa ke nama. Modimo o se phethile ka go roma Morwa wa
it was weak through the flesh. God fulfilled it by sending his

gagwe ka sebopego sa nama ya sebe, gore sebe sa nameng se
Son in the image of the flesh of sin, so that the sin of the flesh be condemned

ahlolelwe go lahlwa; gore re phethegelwe ke tshwanelo, ge re
to be thrown away; so that it be fulfilled for us properly if we throw away

lahla tsela ya nama, ra upša ra ya ka ya Moya.
the way of the flesh, and we rather walk in the way of the Spirit.

- - - - - - - - - - - - - - -

Ka ge re dumela go Jesu Kriste re tseba gore re na le Moya wo
Because we believe in Jesus Christ we know that we have the Holy

Mokgethwa wo o laolago maphelo a rena o re fago bophelo. Moya
Spirit who controls our lives and gives us life. The Holy

wo Mokgethwa woo o re hunolotše dibeng tše molao o re rutago.
Spirit freed us from the sin about which the law instructs us.

Bjale re tseba gore ge re dira dibe re ipiletša lehu. Molao o
Now we know that if we commit sin we call death to us. The law could

be o sa kgone go re lokolla dibeng, ka ge re le batho ba nama
not free us from sin, and because we are people of flesh we could not live

re be re sa kgone go phela gabotse ka mo molao o re laolago ka gona.
right according to the law that governs us.

Eupša Modimo o re diretše seo molao o bego o sa kgona go se dira.
But God did for us what the law could not do.

Modimo o re pholosïitše sebeng seo ka go re romela
God freed us from that sin by sending us his

Morwa wa gagwe, a tla ka sebopego sa nama bjalo ka rena gore e
Son, and he came in the image of flesh like us so that he

tle e be sehlabelo. Ka lebaka leo molao ga o sa re buša o
could be a sacrifice. Therefore the law does no longer rule us,

fedišitšwe mo bophelong bja rena ka gore bjale ga re sa le ba
it has been done away with in our lives since we are no longer of the

nama; re bušwa ke Moya wo Mokgethwa.
flesh; we are now ruled by the Holy Spirit.

Zulu

Ngokuba umthetho kaMoya wokuphila okuKristu Jesu ungikhululile
Because the law of the living Spirit which is with Christ Jesus freed

emthethweni wesono nowokufa. Ngokuba lokho okwehlula umthetho,
me from the law of sin and death. Since that which the law

ngokuba ungenamandla ngenxa yenyama, wakwenza uNkulunkulu
conquered because it had no power because of the flesh caused that God by

ngokuthuma iNdodana yakhe ifana nenyama yesono, nangenxa yesono
sending his Son became like the flesh of sin, and because of sin

walahla isono enyameni, ukuze umyalo womthetho ungcwaliseke
he threw away the sin in the flesh, so that the command of the law be fulfilled

kithina esingahambi ngokwenyama kepha ngokukaMoya.
for us who do not walk according to the flesh but according to the Spirit.

- - - - - - - - - - - - - - - -

ngoba uMoya Oyingewele obusa impilo yethu nosinika impilo ngoba
For the Holy Spirit, who rules our lives and gives us life because

sikholwa kuJesu Krestu, wasikhulula ezonweni zethu, umthetho
we believe in Jesus Christ, freed us from sin of which the law teaches

osifindisa ngazo ukuba nxa sona ziyosilethela ukufa. Umthetho
us that if we sin it means death to us. The law cannot

awunakusikhulula ngoba singabantu sibuthaka ngokwemvelo ukuba
free us because we are human and weak by nature to follow

silandele umthetho ngokugewele. Kepha uNkulunkulu usenzele
the law in a complete way. But God does for us what the law

esingasoze sikwenzelwe ngumthetho. UNkulunkulu wajezisa kano
can never do for us. God condemned Sin in our

empilweni yethu ngokuthumela indodana yakhe ukuba ibe ngumuntis
lives by sending his Son to become a human like us

njengathi nokuthi izinikele ezonweni ukuze okudingwa umthetho
and gave himself for sin so that what the law requires

kube yisibonakaliso empilweni yethu ngoba singaphili
may be seen in our lives when we live not according to

ngokwemvelo kepha ngokukhokhelwa nguMoya Oyingewele.
our nature but by the Holy Spirit leading us.

Tswana

Gonne molaõ oa Mõea oa botshelõ mo go Keresete Yesu o nkgolotse
For the law of the Spirit of life in Christ Jesus freed

mo molaõn oa boleo le oa losho. Gonne se molaõ o no o
me from the law of sin and death. For what the law

retelèlwa ke go se diha, ka go bo o le bokõa kaha nameñ, Modimo
could not do because it is weak in the flesh, God

oa sekisa boleo mo nameñ ka go roma Morwa õna a le mo chwanoñ
judged sin in the flesh by sending his Son in the image of

ea nama e e leohañ, a bile a le setlhabèlèlõ sa boleo: Gore se
sinful flesh, and in addition he was the sacrifice for sin: So that what

molaõ o se lõpañ se tlè se dihalè mo go rona, ba re sa tsamaeeñ
the law requires may happen in us, who walk not in the

kaha nameñ, me e le kaha moeeñ.
flesh, but in the Spirit.

- - - - - - - - - - - - - - - -

Gonne Mowa o o Boitshepo o o laolang botshelo jwa rona gape o o
For the Holy Spirit who rules our lives and gives us life

re nayang botshelo ka gonne re dumela mo go Jesu Keresete, o re
because we believe in Jesus Christ, freed us from sin of

golotse mo dibeng tse molao o re rutang gore fa re dira dibe re
which the law teaches us that if we sin we will

tla swa. Molao o ne o retelelwa ke go re golola ka gonne re
die. The law could not free us because we lacked power

tlhoka thata ka ntlha ya gore re le ba nama mme ga re kgone go
since we are of the flesh and we cannot free

ikgolola molaong. Fela Modimo o re diretse tse di reteletseng
ourselves by the law. But God did for us what the law

molao. Modimo o ile o atlhola boleo mo botshelong jwa rona ka
could not do. God condemned sin in our lives by sending

go romela Morwaa-ona gore e nne motho jaaka rona. Le gore e
his Son to become a human being like us. And also that

nne setlhabelo sa dibe, gore tse molao o neng o di laola, o sa
he could be a sacrifice to sin so that what the law controlled

tlhole o di laola mo botshelong jwa rona ka gonne re sa tshele
it could no longer control in our lives because we no longer live according

ka nama, fela re tshela ka tse Mowa o di dirang mo go rona.
to the flesh, but we live according to what the Spirit does in us.

Index of Scripture References